Unhinged History

The Most Wild, Absurd & Unfiltered Short
Stories That Were NOT Taught in School.
Over 88 Interesting & Hilarious True Stories
for Curious Kids

Cozy Nook Books

TABLE OF CONTENTS

INTRODUCTION

Forget dusty textbooks. Forget boring dates. Forget everything you *think* you know about history.

Seriously. Toss it out.

Because the history you learned in school? That was the filtered version. The neat-and-tidy version. The version where everyone acts... well, *normal.*

But let's be real. Was everyone in the past walking around being perfectly sensible all the time? No way! History is jam-packed with moments so weird, so wild, so unbelievably *bonkers* that they sound completely made up. We're talking about leaders who made decisions that would get you kicked out of a group chat, wars starting over the *stupidest* things imaginable, and animals somehow causing mayhem wherever they went.

This isn't your grandma's history book (unless your grandma is secretly awesome). This is *Unhinged History.*

Think about it. Did your teacher ever tell you about the time an entire army declared war on... *birds?* **And lost?** Or about the emperor who loved his horse so much he tried to make it a high-ranking government official? What about the time a major city was flooded not with water, but with *beer?* Or *molasses?*

Yeah. *Didn't think so.*

These are the stories that usually get swept under the rug. Maybe they're too embarrassing, too ridiculous, or just too unhinged for the serious history books. But that's exactly why they're amazing! Kids and teens are naturally drawn to stuff that breaks the mold—anything weird, strange, or different grabs attention. This book is a deep dive into those moments, the historical happenings that make you slap your forehead and yell, "Wait, that *actually* happened?!".

We scoured the past for the most mind-blowing, laugh-out-loud, and head-scratching true tales we could find. We're talking:

- **Ridiculous Wars and Military Mishaps:** Forget epic strategies; think epic fails. Wars started over buckets, stray dogs, and even insults about ears. We've got tales of weapons so weird they sound like bad sci-fi (bat bombs, anyone?), and soldiers who forgot the war was even happening for hundreds of years.

- **Leaders Who Were Clearly Losing It:** Power does weird things to people. Like, "declare war on the sea god" weird. Or "ban sneezing" weird. Or "put your enemies on trial after they're already dead" weird. Get ready to meet rulers whose grip on reality was... questionable, to say the least.

- **Animal Chaos:** Sometimes, animals steal the show. Like the bear that officially joined the army and carried ammo. Or the bunnies that basically staged a White House takeover. Or the time throwing pots of angry snakes was considered a legitimate naval tactic. History's got some wild creature features.

- **Government Genius (Spoiler: Often Not Genius):** Bureaucracy can be bizarre. We've found stories of governments trying to weaponize *cats*, accidentally causing snake infestations while trying to get rid of snakes, banning popular sports, and building things so badly they became legendary failures (looking at you, Boston's Big Dig). Sometimes, the plan is just... wow.

- **Cultural Crazes:** People are weird. Like, "thousands of people spontaneously start dancing and can't stop" weird. Or "accepting fake money printed by a guy who declared himself Emperor of America" weird. Or "fighting a rebellion over the right to wear puffy pants" weird. We'll look at trends, fads, and moments of mass hysteria that prove humans have always been wonderfully strange.

- **And Other Just Plain Wild Stories:** From disastrous dinner parties to people surviving the impossible, from epic heists involving maple syrup to bizarre job titles you won't believe were real—we've got a whole section dedicated to the historical weirdness that just doesn't fit anywhere else.

This book is designed like a highlight reel of history's most WTF moments. Fast-paced, shocking, and seriously funny. Forget boring lectures; think bite-sized blasts of unbelievable truth. Each story is short, punchy, and guaranteed to make you ask, "Why didn't they teach us *this* in school?!".

So, buckle up. Prepare to have your mind blown. History is way stranger, funnier, and more unhinged than you ever imagined. Let's dive into the chaos.

PART 1:

RIDICULOUS WARS AND MILITARY MISHAPS

Alright, let's talk about war. Usually, it's painted as this super serious thing with brave soldiers, brilliant generals, and world-changing consequences. And yeah, sometimes it is. But other times? Other times it's just... weird. Like, really, *really* weird.

Sometimes, wars are started for the dumbest reasons imaginable. Sometimes, the battle plans are so crazy they sound like they were cooked up during a fever dream. And sometimes, the armies involved looked less like crack troops and more like a clumsy disaster waiting to happen.

This section is all about those moments. We're diving headfirst into the military mishaps, the strategic faceplants, and the conflicts so absurd they make you wonder if someone slipped laughing gas into the water supply. Forget epic charges and heroic last stands for a minute; we're talking about fighting against birds (and losing), declaring war on the ocean, weaponizing bats, and fighting over things like stray dogs and wooden buckets.

Get ready to explore the side of military history that's less "Band of Brothers" and more "Dude, Where's My Tank?". These are the stories of unhinged decisions, unbelievable incompetence, and outcomes so strange they have to be true.

THE GREAT EMU WAR:
HUMANITY VS. BIG BIRDS (SPOILER: THE BIRDS WON)

Location: Australia **Year:** 1932

Picture this: Australia, 1932. The Great Depression is hitting hard, farmers are struggling, and things are looking grim. But the farmers in Western Australia have an extra problem. A big, feathery problem. We're talking about **emus**.

Not just a few emus, mind you. An army. An estimated **20,000** of these giant, flightless birds decided that the farmers' freshly planted wheat fields looked like an all-you-can-eat buffet. They swarmed the farmlands, trampling fences, gobbling crops, and generally making a massive nuisance of themselves. These weren't just annoying pests; they were like an invading army threatening the farmers' way of life.

The desperate farmers, many of them former soldiers from World War I, appealed to the government for help. They knew how to handle enemies with guns, right? So, they asked for... machine guns. And the Minister of Defence, Sir George Pearce, thought, "Sure, why not? Good target practice for our boys, and we get rid of these feathered menaces. What could possibly go wrong?"

Famous last words.

Major G.P.W. Meredith of the Royal Australian Artillery was put in charge, leading a crack team of two soldiers armed with two Lewis machine guns and 10,000 rounds of ammunition. Their mission: wage war on the emus. The media hyped it up. This was humanity versus the birds. Easy win, right?

Wrong.

The first attempt was a disaster. The soldiers spotted a flock of about 50 emus. They set up the guns, took aim, and opened fire. Did the emus panic and scatter? Nope. They split into small groups and ran *around* the bullets with surprising speed and agility. Major Meredith reportedly complained that the emus were like tanks, saying, "If we had soldiers who could absorb bullets like these birds, we could take on any army."

They tried ambushes. They tried chasing them in trucks (which was bumpy and made aiming impossible). Nothing worked. The emus were too fast, too smart, and too spread out. After firing thousands of rounds, the official kill count was laughably low—maybe a few hundred birds. Some reports even claimed it took *ten* bullets per confirmed kill. The emus seemed to have uncanny tactical awareness, often having a leader bird watch for danger while the others ate.

The press had a field day, mocking the military's failure. Headlines screamed about the victorious emu army. After about a month of embarrassment and wasted ammo, the military withdrew. The "Great Emu War" was over.

The final score? Emus: 1, Australian Army: 0.

The government later tried bounty systems, which proved slightly more effective, but the legend of the Emu War lives on as a hilarious testament to the fact that sometimes, nature (especially big, fast birds) just refuses to cooperate with military planning. It remains one of history's most bizarre conflicts—a full-scale military operation against birds, where the birds decisively won.

THE LAST SAMURAI:
30 YEARS HIDING IN THE JUNGLE

Location: Lubang Island, Philippines **Year:** War ended 1945, Soldier surrendered 1974

World War II ended in August 1945. Japan surrendered. The world began to rebuild. But someone forgot to tell Lieutenant Hiroo Onoda.

Okay, that's not entirely fair. People *tried* to tell him. But Onoda, a Japanese intelligence officer stationed on the small island of Lubang in the Philippines, had one final order burned into his brain: **"Do not surrender. Do not die by your own hand. Hold your post."** And he took that order *very* seriously.

When Allied forces took Lubang near the end of the war, Onoda and a few other soldiers melted into the dense jungle. They saw the leaflets dropped from planes announcing Japan's surrender, but they thought it was enemy propaganda—a trick to lure them out. They heard loudspeaker announcements, but dismissed them as fake. They even found newspapers left by islanders, but figured the stories about peace were just clever enemy propaganda.

For Onoda, the war was still on.

For the next **29 years**, he and his dwindling group lived in the jungle, surviving on bananas, coconuts, and stolen livestock from local farmers (who they still believed were the enemy). They patched up their aging uniforms, kept their rifles meticulously clean, and occasionally conducted "guerrilla raids" on island villages, convinced they were disrupting enemy supply lines. Several firefights broke out over the decades, leading to the deaths of Onoda's companions and several Filipino locals. He was a ghost, a relic of a war long finished, still fighting battles in his own mind.

Search parties were sent from Japan. His family recorded messages, pleading for him to come home. More leaflets were dropped, including photos and letters from his family. Nothing worked. Onoda was convinced it was all an elaborate hoax. He was waiting for his commanding officer to return and officially relieve him of duty.

Finally, in 1974, a young Japanese adventurer named Norio Suzuki set out specifically to find Lieutenant Onoda. And incredibly, he did. Suzuki found the aging soldier still patrolling the jungle. But Onoda *still* wouldn't surrender. Not without orders from his commander.

Suzuki returned to Japan with photos proving Onoda was alive. The Japanese government located Onoda's former commanding officer, Major Yoshimi Taniguchi, who was now an old man working in a bookstore. They flew Major Taniguchi to Lubang.

In March 1974, Major Taniguchi walked into the jungle, wearing his old uniform, and formally read out the orders relieving Lieutenant Onoda of his duties and commanding him to lay down his arms.

Only then, after nearly three decades of hiding and fighting a phantom war, did Hiroo Onoda finally accept that World War II was over. He emerged from the jungle, lean and weathered but still wearing his tattered imperial army uniform. He formally surrendered his sword to the Philippine President.

He had held his post, just as ordered, for 29 years after the war ended. It's a mind-boggling story of loyalty and duty taken to the absolute extreme; a lonely war fought long after peace had been declared.

CALIGULA VS. THE SEA GOD: WHEN AN EMPEROR DECLARED WAR ON WATER

Location: Roman Empire (specifically, the English Channel) **Year:** 40 A.D.

Roman Emperors are famous for being a bit... extra. But Emperor Caligula? He took "extra" to a whole new level. We're talking about the guy who supposedly tried to make his horse a consul (a high-ranking political position). But perhaps his most baffling moment was when he decided to declare war on the sea. Yes, the actual ocean.

Caligula fancied himself a great military commander, even though he had zero experience. He decided he needed a big win to make himself look good, so he planned an invasion of Britain. He marched his legions—thousands of heavily armed, highly trained soldiers—all the way from Rome to the northern coast of Gaul (modern-day France), right across the English Channel from Britain.

The troops were assembled. The ships were (supposedly) ready. The stage was set for a grand invasion.

And then... nothing. Caligula just... stopped.

Why? Nobody knows for sure. Maybe the weather was bad. Maybe the troops were mutinous (they weren't exactly thrilled about crossing the dangerous channel). Maybe Caligula just got bored. Whatever the reason, the invasion was off.

But Caligula couldn't go back to Rome empty-handed. He needed spoils of war! He needed proof of his "victory"! So, according to the ancient historian Suetonius (who, admittedly, loved juicy gossip), Caligula did something utterly bizarre.

He ordered his legions to deploy in full battle formation **on the beach,** facing the waves. He had them draw their swords, ready their javelins, and prepare for combat. Their enemy? **Neptune,** the Roman god of the sea.

Yes, Caligula literally commanded his army to attack the water.

Imagine the scene: Thousands of tough Roman soldiers, veterans of brutal campaigns, standing ankle-deep in the surf, stabbing and slashing at the incoming waves as if fighting a liquid monster. The trumpets probably sounded the charge. Maybe Caligula was shouting orders from a safe distance. It is peak absurdity.

But wait, it gets weirder. After the "battle" against the waves, Caligula declared victory over Neptune! And what do victorious armies do? They collect spoils! So, he ordered his soldiers to gather **seashells** from the beach. These shells, he proclaimed, were the "plunder of the ocean," the tribute taken from the defeated sea god.

He then marched his army back toward Rome, carrying wagonloads of seashells as proof of his glorious conquest. He even started planning a "triumph," a massive victory parade through Rome, to celebrate his defeat of... water.

Historians still debate how much of this story is true and how much is exaggeration by writers who hated Caligula (and many did). Did he *really* think he fought Neptune? Or was it some strange punishment for mutinous troops, forcing them to do something humiliating? Or maybe a bizarre attempt to gather materials (some shells produced valuable dye)?

We'll likely never know the full story. But the image of Roman legions attacking the English Channel and gathering seashells as war booty is just too perfectly unhinged not to remember. It stands as one of history's ultimate examples of a leader completely losing the plot.

BAT BOMBS:
WEAPONIZING FLYING MAMMALS IN WWII

Location: USA (Development), Japan (Intended Target) **Year:** 1940s

World War II saw some truly innovative and terrifying weapons: atomic bombs, jet engines, guided missiles. And then there were... **bat bombs**.

No, that's not a typo. The United States military genuinely spent millions of dollars (a huge sum back then) on a top-secret project to strap tiny incendiary bombs to live bats and drop them over Japanese cities.

The idea sounds like something out of a cartoon, but it came from a Pennsylvania dentist named Lytle S. Adams. Adams was vacationing in New Mexico, home to the Carlsbad Caverns and millions of bats. He was also fuming about the Japanese attack on Pearl Harbor. Watching the bats emerge at dusk, an idea struck him: Bats can fly, they roost in dark, hidden places (like the eaves of buildings), and there are *millions* of them. What if you could attach tiny fire-starting devices to them?

He pitched the idea directly to the White House in 1942. Surprisingly, President Franklin D. Roosevelt, known for embracing unconventional ideas, approved it. The project, codenamed "Project X-Ray," was greenlit.

The plan was wild:

1. Capture millions of Mexican free-tailed bats.

2. Develop tiny, timed incendiary bombs, light enough for a bat to carry.

3. Cool the bats into hibernation so they could be packed into special bomb casings (each holding over 1,000 bats).

4. Fly these bat-filled bombs over Japanese cities at night.

5. Deploy parachutes on the casings, which would open mid-air, allowing the bats to warm up, wake up, and fly away.

6. The bats would naturally seek dark places to roost—attics, eaves, factories, warehouses, mostly made of wood and paper in Japanese cities at the time.

7. The timers on their tiny bombs would go off, starting thousands of small fires simultaneously across the city, overwhelming firefighters and causing chaos.

Scientists, including the inventor of napalm, Louis Fieser, were brought in. They developed a tiny 17-gram napalm bomb with a timer. They designed the special refrigerated carriers. They tested different bat species.

But working with live animals proved... tricky.

During one test at Carlsbad Army Airfield Auxiliary Air Base in New Mexico, some armed bats escaped. They flew off and dutifully roosted under a fuel tank and in the rafters of a nearby hangar and general's barracks. The timers went off as planned, and the bats successfully burned the entire test range to the ground. Oops. Project X-Ray had accidentally bombed itself.

Despite this fiery setback (or perhaps because it proved the concept worked?), the project continued. They moved testing to a safer location. By 1944, they had ironed out many kinks.

However, the project was slow and expensive. Meanwhile, another top-secret weapon project was making much faster progress: the Manhattan Project, developing the atomic bomb. The military decided the A-bomb was a more promising (and terrifyingly effective) path to ending the war.

Project X-Ray was officially cancelled in 1944, having cost around $2 million. The bat bombs were never deployed in combat.

It remains one of the strangest "what ifs" of World War II—a bizarre, almost comical plan that came surprisingly close to becoming a reality. Imagine trying to explain *that* one in the history books: ending the war with bomb-carrying bats.

THE WAR OF THE STRAY DOG:
WHEN A RUNAWAY PUP NEARLY CAUSED A BALKAN WAR

Location: Greece-Bulgaria Border **Year:** 1925

International relations can be tense. Borders can be sensitive places. Sometimes, all it takes is one small spark to ignite a major conflict. In 1925, that spark wasn't an assassination or a political dispute. It was a dog.

Okay, maybe it wasn't *just* the dog, but the dog definitely kicked things off.

At the time, relations between Greece and Bulgaria were already pretty frosty. There was bad blood left over from previous Balkan Wars, ongoing disputes about territory and minority populations, and a general atmosphere of suspicion and hostility along their shared border. Soldiers on both sides were jumpy.

The incident happened near the border town of Petrich in Bulgaria. According to one popular version of the story (details vary slightly), a Greek soldier was stationed at a border post. His dog, perhaps chasing a rabbit or just feeling adventurous, ran across the border into Bulgarian territory.

The soldier, not wanting to lose his furry friend (or maybe just bored), ran after the dog. A Bulgarian border guard saw the Greek soldier crossing the border—a violation of territory!—and shouted at him. Things escalated quickly. Shots were fired. The Greek soldier was killed.

Boom. International incident.

The Greek government, led by the rather dictator-ish General Theodoros Pangalos, was furious. They saw this not as a misunderstanding over a dog, but as Bulgarian aggression. They issued an ultimatum to Bulgaria: punish those responsible, apologize formally, and pay reparations.

Bulgaria expressed regret over the soldier's death but argued the Greek soldier had crossed the border first. They proposed a joint investigation. Greece rejected this.

Instead, Greece launched a full-scale invasion of Bulgaria. Greek troops poured across the border, occupied several Bulgarian villages, and headed toward the town of Petrich. It looked like a new Balkan war was about to erupt, all because a soldier chased his dog.

Panic spread. Bulgaria appealed to the League of Nations (the precursor to the United Nations), pleading for help to stop the invasion. Thankfully, the League acted quickly. They condemned the Greek invasion and ordered an immediate ceasefire and withdrawal of Greek troops. They sent military attachés to observe the situation.

Facing international pressure and the threat of sanctions, Greece reluctantly complied. They pulled their troops back. The League of Nations investigated, ultimately blaming Greece for the escalation and ordering them to pay compensation to Bulgaria for the invasion.

The "War of the Stray Dog" (also known as the Petrich Incident) lasted about ten days. Several dozen soldiers and civilians were killed on both sides. It was a brief but bloody reminder of how easily simmering tensions could boil over, and how even the smallest, most mundane event—like a dog chasing its tail across an imaginary line—could almost trigger a full-blown war between nations. It's a total historical facepalm showing the ridiculous things that can happen when national pride meets itchy trigger fingers.

THE WAR OF THE OAKEN BUCKET:
STEALING KITCHENWARE SPARKS A MEDIEVAL MELEE

Location: Northern Italy (Modena vs. Bologna) **Year:** 1325

People have fought wars over land, religion, power, and resources. But have they ever fought a war over... a bucket?

Yes. Yes, they have.

Welcome to medieval Italy, a place full of rival city-states constantly squabbling with each other. Two of these rivals were Modena and Bologna. Think of them like intense crosstown high school rivals, but with castles, knights, and a lot more pointy objects. They belonged to opposing political factions (Ghibellines supporting the Holy Roman Emperor vs. Guelphs supporting the Pope) and basically looked for any excuse to fight.

In 1325, tensions were already high. Then came the bucket incident.

According to legend (and let's be honest, the best stories have a bit of legend), a small group of soldiers from Modena decided to sneak into the rival city of Bologna. Was it a daring military raid? A strategic reconnaissance mission? Nope. They snuck into the city center and **stole a wooden bucket** from the main well.

Why? Maybe as a prank. Maybe as a trophy. Maybe just because they could. Whatever the reason, they grabbed the oaken bucket and legged it back to Modena, probably laughing their heads off.

The Bolognese were *not* amused. This wasn't just any bucket; it was *their* bucket, from *their* city well! It was a symbol, an insult! They demanded Modena return the bucket immediately.

Modena refused. They displayed the stolen bucket proudly, like a championship trophy. "Come and get it," they basically taunted.

That was it. The final straw. Bologna declared war on Modena. Over a bucket.

Okay, historians will tell you the bucket wasn't the *only* reason. There were decades of political rivalry, border disputes, and general bad blood. The bucket theft was more like the match that lit the powder keg. But still! The immediate trigger for mobilization was a piece of stolen kitchenware.

The two cities mustered their armies. Thousands of men prepared for battle. This wasn't just a small skirmish; it led to the Battle of Zappolino, one of the largest battles of the Italian Middle Ages. Sources say around 30,000 infantry and 2,000 cavalry clashed just outside Bologna.

Surprisingly, Modena, though outnumbered, scored a decisive victory. They chased the Bolognese forces back into their city, taunting them from outside the walls. Did they get Bologna to surrender? No. Did they settle their political differences? No. Did they finally return the bucket? Absolutely not!

The war eventually fizzled out, as many medieval conflicts did, without a clear resolution. But Modena kept the bucket.

And they *still* have it.

Seriously. The actual (or at least, believed to be actual) bucket stolen in 1325 is still proudly displayed in Modena's town hall, the Palazzo Comunale, housed within the bell tower called Torre della Ghirlandina. It sits there as a bizarre trophy from a war sparked, in part, by its own theft nearly 700 years ago. It's a wooden reminder that sometimes, the reasons for war are utterly, ridiculously petty.

The High-Tech Toilet
That Sank a Nazi Submarine

Location: North Sea, off the coast of Scotland **Year:** April 1945

Submarines are marvels of engineering, designed to withstand immense pressure and operate in stealth deep beneath the waves. But sometimes, even the most advanced technology can be defeated by the most basic human need: using the toilet.

Meet U-1206, a state-of-the-art German Type VIIC U-boat launched late in World War II. These subs were packed with advanced tech for the time, including a new kind of high-pressure toilet designed to work even when the submarine was deep underwater. Older subs had to surface or be at shallow depths to flush, which was obviously dangerous in enemy waters. This new toilet was supposed to be a game-changer.

There was just one problem: It was incredibly complicated.

Operating this deepwater commode involved a precise sequence of opening and closing various valves to manage the high pressure difference between the inside of the sub and the ocean outside. Get the sequence wrong, and instead of flushing waste *out*, you could end up flushing seawater *in*. Violently. There were specially trained technicians onboard just to operate the toilets.

In April 1945, U-1206 was on its very first combat patrol, lurking deep beneath the North Sea near Scotland. The commander, Kapitänleutnant Karl-Adolf Schlitt, needed to use the facilities. Maybe the trained toilet technician was busy. Maybe Schlitt thought, "How hard can it be?" Whatever the reason, he decided to operate the complex flushing mechanism himself.

He got the sequence wrong.

Instead of a clean flush, a powerful jet of seawater, mixed with sewage from the holding tank, blasted back into the submarine's toilet compartment. Water began flooding in uncontrollably.

Panic! The flood quickly reached the submarine's massive batteries located directly below the toilet compartment. When saltwater hits lead-acid batteries like those, it creates a chemical reaction that releases **chlorine gas**—deadly poisonous gas.

Suddenly, the state-of-the-art submarine was filling with toxic gas and flooding with seawater. Schlitt had no choice. He had to order the U-boat to surface immediately, right in the middle of enemy-patrolled waters, just to save his crew from suffocating or drowning inside their own technologically advanced tin can.

As soon as U-1206 breached the surface, it was spotted by British patrol planes. Bombs rained down. With the submarine already crippled by the toilet incident and now under attack, Schlitt ordered the crew to scuttle (intentionally sink) the U-boat and abandon ship.

Several crew members died during the surfacing and subsequent attack, but most, including Schlitt, were captured by the British.

And so, one of Nazi Germany's advanced U-boats met its end not in a glorious naval battle, but because its commander couldn't figure out how to use the fancy new toilet. It's perhaps the most embarrassing (and fatal) plumbing mishap in military history—a submarine sunk by its own loo. Talk about going down the drain.

THE 335-YEAR WAR:
THE CONFLICT EVERYONE FORGOT TO END

Location: Netherlands vs. Isles of Scilly (off the coast of Cornwall, UK) **Years:** 1651–1986

Wars usually end with battles, treaties, surrenders, or at least someone remembering they were fighting. But what if a war just... fizzled out? What if everyone involved simply forgot about it for centuries?

Let's look at the strange story of the Three Hundred and Thirty-Five Years' War between the Netherlands and the Isles of Scilly. It's officially one of the longest wars in history, and also one with zero casualties and zero actual fighting after the initial declaration.

Here's how this historical head-scratcher happened:

It all goes back to the English Civil War (1642–1651). The Parliamentarians (led by Oliver Cromwell) were kicking butt against the Royalists (supporting King Charles I and later II). The Royalist navy was eventually pushed back to the Isles of Scilly, a small archipelago off the southwestern tip of England.

The Netherlands, meanwhile, had been allied with the Parliamentarians. The Dutch navy suffered some heavy losses from the Royalist fleet operating out of Scilly. Fed up, the Dutch sent Admiral Maarten Tromp to the islands in 1651 to demand reparations from the Royalists for the damage to their ships.

The Royalists basically said, "Nope."

So, Admiral Tromp, likely exceeding his authority a bit, **declared war**. But *only* on the Isles of Scilly, since the rest of England was controlled by their Parliamentarian allies. It was a very specific, localized declaration of war.

Just a few months later, in June 1651, the Parliamentarian fleet showed up and forced the Royalist navy on Scilly to surrender. The English Civil War effectively ended soon after. The Dutch threat to the tiny islands vanished almost as soon as it appeared.

And then... everyone just forgot about the declaration of war.

The Dutch admiral sailed away. The English sorted out their own internal conflicts. The Isles of Scilly went back to being quiet, windswept islands. Nobody ever fired a shot in anger between the Dutch and the Scillonians. No peace treaty was ever signed because, frankly, nobody thought it was necessary. The "war" was a non-event, overshadowed by bigger conflicts.

Fast forward **335 years**.

In 1985, Roy Duncan, a historian and Chairman of the Isles of Scilly Council, was poking around in old records. He stumbled upon the documents detailing the Dutch declaration of war from 1651. He realized, with a jolt, that technically, according to international law, the Isles of Scilly and the Netherlands were *still at war*. Nobody had ever officially called it off!

Duncan wrote to the Dutch Embassy in London, pointing out this centuries-old historical oversight. The Dutch, likely amused and slightly baffled, checked their own records and confirmed it.

So, in 1986, the Dutch Ambassador Rein Huydecoper traveled to the Isles of Scilly. In a friendly ceremony, he met with Chairman Duncan and they officially signed a peace treaty, finally ending the "war" that had been technically ongoing since 1651.

Ambassador Huydecoper joked that it must have been harrowing for the Scillonians "to know we could have attacked at any moment."

And so ended the longest, most peaceful war in history—a conflict that lasted three and a third centuries simply because everyone forgot it had ever started.

Kidnapped by Pirates?
Just Wait 'Til Caesar Gets Revenge

Location: Aegean Sea **Year:** 75 B.C.

Before Julius Caesar was *the* Julius Caesar—dictator of Rome, conqueror of Gaul, salad namesake—he was a young, ambitious nobleman trying to make his way in the world. And like many young people trying to find themselves, he decided to travel abroad to study. But his gap year took a slightly more dramatic turn than most.

Around 75 B.C., when Caesar was in his mid-twenties, he was sailing across the Aegean Sea heading toward Rhodes to study oratory (public speaking—a key skill for Roman politicians). Unfortunately for him, the Aegean was crawling with pirates. Cilician pirates, to be exact, and they were notorious. Caesar's ship was captured, and he found himself a prisoner.

The pirates, realizing they had captured a Roman nobleman, figured they could ransom him for a hefty sum. They demanded 20 talents of silver—a huge amount of money (think millions of dollars today).

Now, most people kidnapped by terrifying pirates would be, well, terrified. They'd keep quiet, hope for the best, maybe cry a little. Not Caesar. According to the historian Plutarch, Caesar *laughed* at the pirates. He told them they clearly didn't know who they'd captured and that he was worth *way* more than 20 talents. He insisted they raise the ransom demand to **50 talents!**

The pirates were probably confused but intrigued. This young Roman had guts.

While waiting for his associates to raise the massive ransom (which took about 38 days), Caesar didn't act like a prisoner. He acted more like he was in charge. He bossed the pirates around, told them when to be quiet so he could sleep, wrote poems and speeches, and made the pirates listen to them (critiquing them if they didn't appreciate his genius), and joined in their games and exercises.

He treated them less like captors and more like... his slightly annoying roommates.

But here's the kicker: Throughout his captivity, Caesar repeatedly and cheerfully told the pirates that as soon as he was released, he would hunt them all down and have them **crucified.**

The pirates probably thought he was joking. A young, unarmed nobleman making threats? Hilarious! They laughed along with him. They seemed to genuinely like their strange, arrogant captive.

Eventually, the 50 talents arrived, paid by cities in Asia Minor where Caesar had connections. The pirates, true to their word (sort of), released Caesar on an island.

Did Caesar breathe a sigh of relief and head straight home? Absolutely not. He had promises to keep.

He immediately went to the nearby port city of Miletus, raised a private fleet of ships, manned them with volunteers, and sailed straight back to the island where the pirates were still hanging out, probably counting their silver. He caught them completely by surprise.

Caesar captured most of the pirates and, more importantly, recovered the 50 talents ransom money (plus the pirates' own loot). He then took his prisoners to the mainland and handed them over to the Roman governor, demanding they be executed as promised.

The governor, however, was a bit greedy and saw a chance to sell the pirates into slavery instead. Caesar wasn't having it. He basically ignored the governor, went to the prison where the pirates were being held, and had every single one of them **crucified,** just like he'd cheerfully promised them while he was their prisoner. (Plutarch adds that because they'd treated him relatively well, Caesar showed a tiny bit of "mercy" by having their throats cut *before* they were crucified, to make their deaths quicker. Thanks, Julius?)

It was a ruthless, decisive, and utterly badass move that cemented Caesar's reputation early on. Don't mess with Caesar. Especially don't kidnap him. He *will* find you, and he keeps his promises.

THE WAR OF JENKINS' EAR:
AN OLD BODY PART SPARKS AN IMPERIAL CONFLICT

Location: Caribbean Sea/North America (Britain vs. Spain) **Years:** 1739–1748

Wars have been fought over land, treasure, religion, and power. But this might be the only major war sparked, at least in name, by a severed body part kept pickled in a jar.

Meet Robert Jenkins, a British merchant sea captain sailing in the Caribbean in the 1730s. This was a time of intense rivalry between Great Britain and Spain, especially over trade in the Americas. Spain claimed vast territories and tried to monopolize trade, while British merchants (some engaging in smuggling, let's be honest) tried to muscle in. Tensions were high.

In 1731, Jenkins' ship, the *Rebecca*, was stopped and boarded near Havana by the Spanish coast guard vessel *La Isabela*. The Spanish commander, Julio León Fandiño, accused Jenkins of smuggling (which he probably was doing). Things got heated. According to Jenkins, Fandiño's men roughed him up, tied him to a mast, and then, in a moment of brutal intimidation, Lieutenant Fandiño personally sliced off **one of Captain Jenkins' ears** with his sword.

As if that wasn't enough, Fandiño supposedly told Jenkins, "Go, and tell your King that I will do the same, if he dares to do the same." (Basically, "Tell your king I'll cut his ear off too if he messes with us.") Then they let Jenkins go, minus one ear.

Now, Jenkins wasn't about to let this go. He carefully **preserved the severed ear**, reportedly pickling it in a bottle of brandy. For the next few years, he tried to get the British government interested, showing his ear (or the story of it) around, but nothing much happened initially.

Fast forward seven years to 1738. Anti-Spanish sentiment in Britain was boiling over due to ongoing trade disputes and incidents at sea. The political opposition wanted war, and they needed a symbol, a rallying cry, a perfect piece of propaganda.

Enter Captain Jenkins and his pickled ear.

He was brought before a committee of the British House of Commons to testify about his ordeal. In a moment of high political theater, Jenkins allegedly produced the shriveled, preserved ear from its jar, holding it aloft for all the politicians to see. He recounted the story of the brutal Spanish attack and the insult to the British King.

Whether he *actually* displayed the ear in Parliament is debated by historians (some think it's a later embellishment), but his story certainly did the trick. Public outrage exploded. Newspapers ran with the story. "Jenkins' Ear" became a symbol of Spanish brutality and arrogance. The pressure for war became immense.

Prime Minister Robert Walpole, who had favored peace, couldn't hold back the tide any longer. In 1739, Great Britain declared war on Spain. While the underlying causes were complex issues of trade and colonial power, the conflict forever became known by the bizarre and gruesome name: **The War of Jenkins' Ear.**

The war itself lasted nine years, involving naval battles in the Caribbean, land campaigns in Florida and Georgia, and eventually merging into the larger War of the Austrian Succession in Europe. Thousands died. Fortunes were spent. Empires clashed.

And it was all kicked off, in the public imagination at least, by one man's pickled ear presented (perhaps) to Parliament. It's a grotesque reminder that sometimes, the symbols of war can be stranger than fiction. What happened to the ear itself? Nobody knows. It vanished from history, leaving only a bizarrely named war in its wake.

THE NEVER-ENDING SIEGE:
21 YEARS TRAPPED IN CANDIA

Location: Candia (modern Heraklion), Crete **Years:** 1648–1669

Sieges in medieval and early modern times could be brutal, drawn-out affairs. Armies would surround a fortified city or castle, cut off its supplies, bombard its walls, and try to starve the defenders into submission. Most sieges lasted weeks or months. Some dragged on for a year or two.

And then there was the Siege of Candia. This wasn't just a siege; it was an entire generation growing up under constant bombardment and blockade. It lasted an almost unbelievable **21 years**.

Candia was the capital of the Kingdom of Candia (modern Crete), which was the most important overseas colony of the Republic of Venice, a wealthy trading empire based in Italy. The mighty Ottoman Empire, based in Turkey, wanted Crete for themselves to control the Eastern Mediterranean. In 1645, the Ottomans landed a huge army on Crete and quickly conquered most of the island. But the capital city, Candia, held out.

In May 1648, the Ottoman army formally began the siege of Candia. They expected it to fall quickly. They were wrong.

Candia was protected by massive, state-of-the-art fortifications built by the Venetians. The defenders, a mix of Venetian soldiers, Cretan locals, and mercenaries from all over Europe (who saw fighting the Ottomans as a Christian duty, or just a job), were determined to hold on. Venice, using its powerful navy, managed to keep supplying the city by sea, breaking through the Ottoman blockade time and again.

What followed was not a quick assault, but two decades of grinding, relentless warfare. The Ottomans dug elaborate trenches, slowly inching closer to the city walls. They launched massive assaults, trying to storm the ramparts, only to be thrown back with horrific casualties. They pounded the city with cannon fire day after day, year after year. Mines were dug under the walls by both sides, leading to desperate, claustrophobic underground battles.

Life inside the besieged city was grim. Buildings were constantly being destroyed by cannonballs. Food was often scarce. Disease was rampant. Yet somehow, the defenders kept fighting. Reinforcements and supplies trickled in from Venice and other European powers who wanted to stop the Ottoman advance. Famous military engineers came to help improve the defenses. Knights from Malta and France joined the fight.

The Ottomans were just as determined. Sultan after Sultan poured resources into the siege. Tens of thousands of Ottoman soldiers died over the years from battle, disease, and accidents in the trenches. It became a matter of pride and imperial ambition. They couldn't back down.

The sheer scale of the conflict was staggering. Historians estimate that over the 21 years, more than 100,000 Ottoman soldiers and perhaps 30,000 defenders and civilians died. Dozens of major assaults were launched. Hundreds of underground mines exploded. It was one of the bloodiest and longest sieges in history.

Finally, in 1669, the exhausted defenders, vastly outnumbered and with their fortifications crumbling beyond repair, negotiated a surrender. The remaining Venetian soldiers and citizens were allowed to leave the city peacefully. After 21 years, 3 months, and 27 days, the Ottoman flag finally flew over Candia.

The siege was a brutal, almost insane display of endurance and determination on both sides. Imagine being born inside those walls, living your entire childhood and teenage years knowing nothing but the sound of cannons and the threat of attack. It's a chilling testament to the extremes of human conflict.

THE FOOTBALL WAR:
WHEN SOCCER RIOTS ESCALATED TO ACTUAL COMBAT

Location: Honduras vs. El Salvador **Year:** 1969

Can a soccer game actually start a war? Well, not exactly. But in 1969, tensions between Honduras and El Salvador were so high that a series of hotly contested World Cup qualifying matches became the trigger for a brief, but bloody conflict known as the **Football War** (or the 100 Hours' War).

The real roots of the conflict were much deeper than soccer. For years, hundreds of thousands of Salvadorans had migrated to neighboring Honduras seeking land and work. This caused resentment among many Hondurans, who felt the immigrants were taking jobs and resources. Land ownership laws were passed in Honduras that disadvantaged the Salvadoran settlers, forcing many to flee back to El Salvador, which was already overpopulated and struggling economically. Nationalism and anti-immigrant sentiment were running dangerously high in both countries.

Into this powder keg dropped the qualifying matches for the 1970 FIFA World Cup. El Salvador and Honduras were drawn to play each other in a three-game series.

Game 1 (June 8, Tegucigalpa, Honduras): Honduras won 1–0. The night before the game, Honduran fans surrounded the hotel where the Salvadoran team was staying, making noise all night—banging drums, setting off fireworks, shouting insults—to prevent the players from sleeping. After the game, there were reports of violence against visiting Salvadoran fans.

Game 2 (June 15, San Salvador, El Salvador): El Salvador won 3–0. This time, it was the Honduran team and their fans who faced harassment. Their hotel was targeted, windows were smashed, and rotten eggs were thrown. The Honduran flag was burned in the stadium. Violence escalated, and Honduran fans were attacked. The Honduran team had to be escorted to and from the stadium under heavy military guard. Reports of attacks on Salvadoran immigrants living in Honduras intensified after this game.

The atmosphere was toxic. Newspapers in both countries fanned the flames with inflammatory headlines and nationalist rhetoric. Diplomatic relations were already strained; now they completely broke down.

Game 3 (June 27, Mexico City - Neutral Ground): This was the playoff decider. El Salvador won 3–2 in extra time, securing their spot in the World Cup. But by now, the soccer results barely mattered. The damage was done.

Back home, reports (some exaggerated, some tragically real) of violence against citizens of the opposing country filled the airwaves. Governments accused each other of atrocities. On July 14, 1969, less than three weeks after the final soccer match, the Salvadoran military launched an invasion of Honduras.

The Salvadoran air force bombed Honduran airfields, and ground troops pushed across the border. The Honduran military fought back. For about four days (roughly 100 hours), the two small Central American nations were engaged in a real war, with tanks, planes, and infantry clashes.

The Organization of American States (OAS) quickly intervened, negotiating a ceasefire that took effect on July 18th. Salvadoran troops eventually withdrew in early August under international pressure.

The war was short, but devastating. Estimates vary, but somewhere between 1,000 and 4,000 people died, mostly Honduran civilians. Tens of thousands of Salvadorans living in Honduras were displaced, forced to flee back to El Salvador, worsening the economic problems there (which contributed to El Salvador's own civil war later).

While the soccer games didn't *cause* the war, they provided the spark that ignited years of underlying tension over land, immigration, and national pride. It's a shocking reminder of how intense sports rivalries, combined with politics and national pride, can explode into deadly real-world violence.

THE ERASED PHARAOH:
TRYING TO DELETE A QUEEN FROM HISTORY

Location: Ancient Egypt **Year:** Reign c. 1478–1458 B.C., Erasure after her death

Imagine being so successful, so powerful, so groundbreaking that your successor tries to pretend you never even existed. That's what happened to Hatshepsut, one of ancient Egypt's most remarkable rulers and one of the few women ever to hold the title of Pharaoh.

Hatshepsut wasn't born to be the main ruler. She was the daughter of one pharaoh (Thutmose I) and the wife of another (her half-brother, Thutmose II). When Thutmose II died young, the throne passed to his infant son, Thutmose III (Hatshepsut's stepson/nephew). Hatshepsut was initially supposed to be the regent, ruling *for* the young king until he came of age.

But Hatshepsut wasn't content being a temporary placeholder. She was ambitious and capable. Within a few years, she did something unprecedented: she declared *herself* Pharaoh, ruling alongside (but really, *as*) the king. This was a huge break from tradition—kingship was overwhelmingly a male role in Egypt.

To legitimize her rule, she went all out. She claimed the god Amun-Ra had declared her the rightful ruler. She adopted the full royal titles and symbols of a male pharaoh. In statues and reliefs, she was often depicted wearing the traditional pharaoh's kilt and false beard, sometimes even with male musculature. She wasn't just a queen; she was a KING.

And she was good at it! Her reign (around 20 years) was one of peace and prosperity. She didn't wage major wars; instead, she focused on building magnificent temples (like her stunning mortuary temple at Deir el-Bahri), restoring monuments, and launching impressive trade expeditions, most famously a voyage to the distant land of Punt (likely somewhere in modern-day Eritrea or Somalia) that brought back incense, ebony, gold, and exotic animals. She was a builder, a diplomat, and an economic powerhouse.

So, what happened after she died (likely from natural causes)?

Her stepson, Thutmose III, finally became the sole Pharaoh, ruling for many decades after her. He became one of Egypt's greatest military leaders, often called the "Napoleon of Egypt." But sometime during his reign (or possibly his son's), a systematic effort began to **erase Hatshepsut from history**.

It was brutal and thorough. Her name was chiseled off monuments and temple walls. Her statues were smashed, torn down, and buried. Reliefs showing her as king were recarved to show her father or husband instead, or simply plastered over. Images of her were systematically destroyed throughout Egypt. They tried to make it seem like her reign never happened, as if Thutmose III had succeeded his father directly.

Why? The exact reasons are debated by Egyptologists. Was it personal revenge by Thutmose III, bitter about being overshadowed for so long? Was it a conservative backlash against the idea of a woman ruling as king, trying to restore traditional male succession and prevent future women from getting similar ideas? Was it simply practical, wanting to solidify Thutmose III's own lineage? Probably a combination of all three.

They wanted to ensure that this anomaly—a woman ruling successfully as pharaoh—was forgotten, wiped from the official record.

For centuries, they largely succeeded. Hatshepsut became a historical footnote, her story obscured. It wasn't until the 19th and 20th centuries, when archaeologists began deciphering hieroglyphs and excavating her temples and buried statues, that the full extent of her reign and the deliberate attempt to erase her came to light.

It's a fascinating case of attempted historical cancellation on a grand scale. Despite the efforts to delete her, Hatshepsut's story survived, pieced back together from the fragments left behind, revealing one of Egypt's most powerful and intriguing rulers—the pharaoh they tried, and failed, to erase.

How a Trip to the Loo Saved Winston Churchill's Life

Location: 10 Downing Street (or nearby Cabinet War Rooms), London, UK **Year:** 1940s (During the Blitz)

Winston Churchill, Britain's iconic Prime Minister during World War II, was known for his stirring speeches, his stubborn defiance of Nazi Germany, and his fondness for cigars and brandy. He was also known for spending a lot of time working late into the night, often from heavily fortified bunkers like the Cabinet War Rooms beneath Whitehall. And according to several accounts, a simple, everyday bodily function might have saved his life during the height of the London Blitz.

The Blitz was the period in 1940 and 1941 when German bombers relentlessly attacked London and other British cities, trying to break the country's morale. Bombs fell night after night, causing widespread destruction and death. Churchill, leading the war effort, was a prime target.

The story goes that one evening, Churchill was working late in his office or study, likely within the Downing Street complex or the nearby underground War Rooms. He was engrossed in paperwork, planning strategy, or perhaps dictating one of his famous speeches. Nature called. Churchill got up from his desk and headed to the lavatory.

He wasn't gone for long, just a few minutes. But in those few minutes, **BAM!** A German bomb scored a direct hit (or a very near miss) on the very room he had just vacated.

The explosion rocked the building, shattering windows, blasting furniture apart, and reducing the area around his desk to rubble. If Churchill had still been sitting there, engrossed in his work, he almost certainly would have been killed or severely injured.

His staff rushed to find him, fearing the worst, only to discover the Prime Minister emerging, perhaps slightly dusty but completely unharmed, from the restroom.

Details of the exact date and location vary slightly in different tellings, as Churchill faced several close calls during the Blitz. One popular version places the incident at 10 Downing Street itself, where a bomb damaged the kitchen and garden rooms in October 1940. Another suggests it happened during a meeting in the Cabinet War Rooms. Churchill himself reportedly recounted such an incident more than once.

Regardless of the precise details, the core story remains the same: A timely trip to the toilet saved Britain's wartime leader from certain death.

It's a darkly humorous, almost absurd twist of fate. The fate of the nation, the course of the war, potentially hanging in the balance, decided by a random bathroom break. It highlights the sheer chance and unpredictability of life during wartime, even for those at the very top. A few minutes earlier or later, and history might have taken a very different course. Sometimes, even Prime Ministers have to thank sheer dumb luck (and a well-timed call of nature) for their survival.

THE ARMY THAT WENT TO WAR AND CAME BACK WITH MORE SOLDIERS

Location: Liechtenstein vs. Prussia/Italy (Austro-Prussian War) **Year:** 1866

Imagine sending your army off to war, bracing for casualties, and then having them return not only unharmed but with... an extra person? That's the delightful, almost unbelievable story of Liechtenstein's last military engagement.

Liechtenstein is a tiny, mountainous principality nestled between Switzerland and Austria. Today, it's known for being wealthy, peaceful, and having no army at all. But back in the mid-19th century, it was part of the German Confederation and had a treaty obligation to provide troops in times of conflict.

In 1866, the Austro-Prussian War broke out. It was a major conflict between the Austrian Empire and its German allies on one side, and Prussia and its allies (including Italy) on the other. Tiny Liechtenstein was obligated to support Austria.

So, Liechtenstein dutifully mustered its army. All **80** of them. Yes, the entire military force of the nation consisted of 80 men. They were sent south to defend the Stelvio Pass in the Italian Alps against a potential Italian invasion, thereby freeing up Austrian troops to fight the Prussians elsewhere.

The 80 Liechtensteiners marched off under the command of their leader (sources vary on his name, possibly Peter Rheinberger). They reached the mountain pass, set up camp, and prepared to defend their post.

And then... nothing happened.

The Italians apparently had no interest in attacking that particular mountain pass. The Liechtenstein army spent their time enjoying the beautiful Alpine scenery, perhaps drinking wine, maybe playing cards. No battles were fought. No shots were fired in anger. Their part of the war was remarkably peaceful.

When the war ended a few weeks later (with Prussia decisively defeating Austria), the 80 soldiers from Liechtenstein packed up their gear and marched home.

When they arrived back in the capital, Vaduz, they were greeted with relief and perhaps a little surprise. Not only had all 80 soldiers returned safely—zero casualties—but they had somehow picked up an extra person along the way!

According to the popular version of the story, they returned with **81** people. Who was the extra guy? Accounts vary. Some say he was an Austrian military liaison officer who decided to come back with them. Others suggest he was an Italian "friend"—perhaps a deserter or just someone who tagged along. One charmingly specific (but possibly legendary) version calls him an "Austrian liaison officer plus an Italian friend."

Whatever the specifics, the core legend remains: The Liechtenstein army went to war with 80 men and returned with 81, suffering no losses whatsoever.

It was Liechtenstein's last ever military engagement. Shortly after this uneventful "war," in 1868, Liechtenstein completely disbanded its army, declaring permanent neutrality. They decided that having an army was just too expensive and, apparently, not very necessary. They haven't had one since (though they maintain a police force).

The story of the 80 soldiers who came back as 81 is a perfect symbol of Liechtenstein's peaceful history—a nation whose final military adventure ended not with bloodshed, but with making a new friend.

PART 2:

LEADERS WHO WERE CLEARLY LOSING IT

Power. It's a heck of a drug. Give someone absolute control over kingdoms, empires, and armies, and sometimes... things go off the rails. Like, *spectacularly* off the rails.

History is littered with leaders who weren't just making bad decisions; they were making decisions so bizarre, so cruel, so utterly unhinged that you have to wonder if anyone ever dared to ask, "Uh, your Majesty... are you feeling okay?"

This section is dedicated to those rulers. The emperors who thought their horses deserved government jobs. The popes who put corpses on trial (yes, really). The kings who thought they were made of glass. The sultans who drowned their entire harems on a whim. The leaders whose grip on reality seemed... slippery, at best.

Forget wise rulers and benevolent monarchs for a moment. We're diving into the reigns of terror, the fits of paranoia, the moments of sheer madness that somehow ended up steering the course of history. These are the stories that prove absolute power doesn't just corrupt; sometimes, it makes people completely lose their minds. Get ready to meet the leaders who were clearly, undeniably, and often terrifyingly losing it.

Emperor Caligula Appoints His Horse... Sort Of
(Roman Empire, ~40 A.D.)

We met Emperor Caligula briefly in the last section when he declared war on the sea. But his eccentricities didn't stop there. His most famous (and maybe exaggerated) weird moment probably involved his favorite horse, Incitatus.

Caligula *loved* this horse. Like, really, *really* loved it. Incitatus wasn't just any horse; he was treated better than most Roman nobles. According to ancient historians like Suetonius and Cassius Dio (who, remember, weren't exactly Caligula's biggest fans), Incitatus had:

- A stable made of marble.

- An ivory manger to eat from.

- Purple blankets (the color reserved for royalty).

- A collar studded with precious jewels.

- His own house, complete with furniture and slaves, to entertain guests!

Caligula would supposedly invite people to dine *with the horse.* Soldiers had to tell everyone nearby to pipe down the night before Incitatus raced, just so the special horse could get his rest.

But the ultimate power move? Caligula supposedly planned to make Incitatus a **consul**. The consuls were the highest elected officials in Rome, basically the co-presidents of the Republic (even under the emperors, the title still held immense prestige). Appointing a horse to this position would be like making your dog Speaker of the House.

Did it actually happen? Probably not fully. Most historians think Caligula never *officially* appointed Incitatus as consul. But did he *say* he was going to? Did he *threaten* the stuffy Roman senators with the ultimate insult of being governed by a horse? Absolutely plausible.

Why would he do such a thing? Was Caligula genuinely insane? Or was it a calculated political move? Maybe he was mocking the senators, showing his contempt for them by suggesting his horse could do their job just as well (or better). Maybe it was a power play, demonstrating that he could do literally *anything* he wanted, no matter how absurd.

Whatever the reason, the story stuck. Caligula and his consul-horse became legendary symbols of imperial excess and madness. Even if Incitatus never actually took office, the fact that Caligula loved his horse *so much* that appointing him to high office seemed remotely possible tells you everything you need to know about how unhinged his reign truly was.

NERO'S GOLDEN HOUSE:
FIDDLING WHILE ROME BURNED? (ROMAN EMPIRE, 64 A.D.)

Emperor Nero is another Roman ruler whose name basically screams "tyrant" and "over-the-top." His most infamous moment is tied to the Great Fire of Rome in 64 A.D., a disaster that destroyed huge swathes of the city. The popular legend, fueled by later historians, paints Nero as a monster who **"fiddled while Rome burned."**

Did he actually play a fiddle (an instrument that didn't exist yet—it would have been a lyre) while watching the city perish? Almost certainly not. Historical accounts say he was actually miles away at his villa in Antium when the fire broke out. When he heard the news, he rushed back to Rome and organized relief efforts, opening his palaces to house the homeless and bringing in food supplies.

So, why the bad rap? Two main reasons:

1. **The Rumors:** Even at the time, rumors flew that Nero had *started* the fire himself. Why? Because he wanted to clear land to build a ridiculously extravagant new palace complex. People whispered that he watched the fire from a tower, singing about the fall of Troy while the city below him turned to ash. True or not, the rumors damaged his reputation badly.

2. **The Golden House (Domus Aurea):** This is where the "losing it" part really kicks in. After the fire conveniently cleared a massive area in the heart of Rome, what did Nero do? He seized a huge chunk of that land (estimated between 100 and 300 acres) to build his dream palace: the **Domus Aurea**, or Golden House.

This wasn't just a palace; it was an architectural ego trip on an epic scale. Imagine:

- Buildings overlaid with gold leaf and studded with gems and mother-of-pearl.

- Rooms with rotating ceilings that showered guests with flowers and perfume.

- An artificial lake, big enough to sail boats on, right in the middle of the city.

- Vast gardens, vineyards, pastures, and even a zoo filled with wild animals.

- A colossal bronze statue of himself (the Colossus of Nero), over 100 feet tall, standing at the entrance.

This opulent monstrosity was built on land where thousands of Romans had lost their homes. While the city struggled to rebuild, Nero poured state resources into his personal pleasure park. It showed incredible arrogance and proved he just didn't care about his people who were suffering.

Whether he started the fire or not, building the Golden House right after was a PR disaster of epic proportions. It cemented his image as a self-absorbed tyrant who cared more about his luxuries than his subjects. The sheer scale and audacity of the Domus Aurea, built literally on the ashes of Rome, is a monument to Nero's unhinged priorities. (Ironically, after Nero's death, the Golden House was largely destroyed or filled in, and the Colosseum was later built on the site of his artificial lake—a public entertainment venue replacing the private indulgence of a hated emperor).

THE CADAVER SYNOD:
THE POPE WHO PUT A CORPSE ON TRIAL (ROME, 897 A.D.)

Okay, buckle up. This one is genuinely one of the most bizarre and gruesome episodes in the history of the Papacy. We're talking about a Pope digging up the rotting corpse of his predecessor, dressing it in sacred robes, propping it up on a throne, and putting it on trial. Seriously.

The late 9th century was a chaotic time in Rome. Various factions were fighting for power, and the Papacy (the office of the Pope) was often caught in the middle, with popes being installed and deposed based on shifting political winds.

Enter Pope Stephen VI. He became Pope in 896 A.D., backed by one powerful Roman family. However, his predecessor, Pope Formosus, had belonged to a rival faction and had made decisions that Stephen VI and his backers really didn't like (including crowning someone they considered an enemy as Holy Roman Emperor).

Stephen VI wasn't content just being Pope; he wanted to utterly destroy Formosus's reputation and legacy. But Formosus was already dead and buried (he'd died about 9 months earlier). Minor inconvenience!

In January 897 A..D, Stephen VI ordered Formosus's body **exhumed** from its grave. The decaying corpse was dressed in full papal vestments (the fancy robes a Pope wears). Then, it was propped up on a throne in the Basilica of St. John Lateran, the Pope's cathedral in Rome.

And then, the trial began. The **Cadaver Synod** (Synod means church council or trial).

Imagine the scene: Pope Stephen VI presiding, cardinals and bishops assembled, and the rotting corpse of Pope Formosus sitting there "facing" his accusers. A young deacon was appointed to stand behind the corpse and "answer" the charges on Formosus's behalf—probably trembling in his sandals.

The charges? Things like perjury, violating church law by switching bishoprics, and ambition. The trial was a complete sham, obviously. The corpse couldn't defend itself. The deacon probably just stammered out whatever answers kept him alive.

The verdict? **Guilty!** (Shocking, right?)

The punishment? Formosus had his title of Pope taken away after he was already dead. All his acts and ordinations were declared invalid (causing chaos for the priests he had ordained). The papal robes were ripped from his corpse. The three fingers he had used for blessings were hacked off.

And then, the mutilated corpse was dragged through the streets of Rome and thrown into the Tiber River. (It was later fished out by monks and secretly reburied).

This disgusting display shocked people even by the chaotic standards of 9th-century Rome. Public opinion turned sharply against Stephen VI. Later that same year, a rival faction rose up, imprisoned Stephen VI, and had him strangled in his cell.

The Cadaver Synod remains a chilling example of political hatred and religious fanaticism taken to an unhinged extreme. Putting a dead body on trial? That's definitely losing the plot.

POPE GREGORY IX VS. CATS:
THE PURR-SECUTION BEGINS (EUROPE, ~1233)

Popes have declared crusades against human enemies, but Pope Gregory IX, in the 13th century, took things a step further. He didn't declare a full-blown "war" on cats, but he did issue a papal bull (an official decree) called **"Vox in Rama"** around 1233 that strongly associated cats, particularly **black cats**, with devil worship and witchcraft. And the consequences were catastrophic for kitties across Europe.

What was going on? This was a time of intense religious fervor and growing fear of heresy (beliefs going against official church doctrine). In Germany, an inquisitor named Conrad of Marburg was zealously hunting down supposed heretics, and he reported finding groups involved in bizarre Satanic rituals. According to these reports (which were likely obtained through torture and were highly suspect), the devil would appear to his worshippers, sometimes in the form of a large black cat. Initiation rites allegedly involved kissing the cat's backside.

Pope Gregory IX took these reports seriously. His "Vox in Rama" decree described these supposed rituals in lurid detail and condemned the participants. While the Pope didn't order people to kill all cats, his announcement definitely made everyone believe cats (especially black ones) were connected to the devil.

The result? A widespread **persecution of cats.**

Across Europe, people began to view cats with suspicion and fear. Seen as companions of witches, agents of Satan, or even the devil in disguise, cats were hunted down and killed in huge numbers. Black cats, in particular, suffered the most. Mass cat killings became disturbingly common in some areas, sometimes incorporated into festivals or religious observances.

This wasn't just bad news for the cats; it might have had devastating consequences for humans, too. Some historians theorize that this drastic reduction in the cat population had an unintended side effect: **It allowed the rat population to explode.**

Why does that matter? Because rats carry fleas, and fleas carry diseases. Most notably, the bubonic plague (the Black Death). While the Black Death pandemic that ravaged Europe a century later (mid-14th century) had complex causes, some scholars suggest that the earlier scarcity of cats—natural predators of rats—might have made Europe more vulnerable when the plague arrived. Fewer cats meant more rats, which meant more plague-carrying fleas, potentially contributing to the devastating spread of the disease.

Did Pope Gregory IX intend to cause a plague by demonizing cats? Of course not. He was acting out of religious conviction and fear of heresy. But his decree, linking furry felines to the forces of darkness, unleashed an unhinged wave of animal cruelty that not only harmed cats but may have inadvertently helped pave the way for one of the deadliest pandemics in human history. Talk about unintended consequences!

King Canute Commands the Tide (England, ~1028)

This is one of those stories that sounds like pure madness, but it might actually be the opposite—a king trying to prove a point about the *limits* of his power, not his insanity. Still, the image is wonderfully absurd.

King Canute the Great was a powerful ruler in the early 11th century. He was a Viking who became King of England, Denmark, and Norway—a vast North Sea empire. He was successful, respected, and probably got tired of people telling him how incredibly powerful he was.

A historian writing about a century later said Canute got tired of his advisors always sucking up and telling him he was all-powerful and could even control nature. He decided to teach them a lesson in humility, with a touch of royal theater.

He ordered his throne to be carried down to the seashore as the tide was coming in. He sat on his throne, surrounded by his fawning nobles, right at the water's edge. Then, with all the authority he could muster, Canute addressed the sea:

"I command you, waves, not to rise onto my land, nor to wet the robes or limbs of your lord!"

He sat there, regal and stern, as if expecting the ocean to obey.

Of course, the tide kept coming in. The waves ignored the royal command completely. They splashed up around the throne, soaking the king's feet and robes. Canute didn't flinch. He let the water rise, proving his point.

Then, he turned to his astonished courtiers and said something like:

"See how empty and worthless the power of kings is! For there is none worthy of the name 'king' except Him whose eternal laws the heavens, the earth, and the sea obey." (Referring to God).

He then supposedly went straight to Winchester Cathedral, took off his crown, and placed it on a crucifix, vowing never to wear it again as a symbol of his own power being nothing compared to God's.

So, was Canute crazy for talking to the waves? No, the story says he put on a clever show to shut up his bootlicking advisors and prove that even powerful kings have to obey nature and God.

However, over the centuries, the story has often been twisted. People forget the *reason* he commanded the waves; they just remember the image of a king arrogantly trying to stop the tide, making him look like a fool who genuinely thought he could control the ocean.

Whether it happened exactly as described or not, the image of King Canute sitting on his throne while the tide rolls in is a classic "unhinged history" moment—either a king wisely demonstrating the limits of power, or a legend misinterpreted into a tale of royal delusion.

King Charles VI:
The Glass King of France
(France, late 14th/early 15th C)

Imagine being terrified that you might shatter into a million pieces at any moment. That was the bizarre reality for King Charles VI of France, whose rule was troubled by worse and worse episodes of mental illness, earning him the nickname "Charles the Mad."

Charles started out okay. He came to the throne as a boy and was initially known as "Charles the Beloved." But in 1392, while leading a military expedition, he suffered his first major psychotic break. Riding through a forest on a hot summer day, a clumsy page accidentally dropped a lance, making a loud clatter. The noise startled the King, who suddenly drew his sword, screamed "Forward against the traitors! They wish to deliver me to the enemy!", and charged wildly at his own men, killing several knights (including a close friend) before his attendants could subdue him.

He lapsed into a coma for days. When he recovered, he didn't remember the incident, but it was the start of a lifelong struggle with mental illness. His episodes became more frequent and more bizarre over the next 30 years.

Sometimes he wouldn't recognize his own wife or children. Sometimes he couldn't remember his own name or that he was King. He would run wildly through the halls of his palace, howling like a wolf. For months at a time, he would refuse to bathe or change his clothes.

But perhaps his most famous delusion was the **"glass delusion."**

During some of his episodes, King Charles VI became convinced that his body was made entirely of **glass**. He was terrified that if someone touched him too roughly, or if he fell, he would shatter into tiny fragments.

Because of this, he refused to let people touch him. He reportedly had iron rods sewn into his clothing to prevent him from breaking if he bumped into something. He would sit motionless for hours, afraid that any sudden movement could cause irreparable damage to his fragile glass body.

Imagine the chaos this caused for the French court and government. The King, the center of all power, was periodically convinced he was a delicate glass figurine. Important decisions were delayed, factions fought for control during his periods of incapacity, and France suffered setbacks in the ongoing Hundred Years' War against England (including the devastating defeat at Agincourt in 1415, which happened during one of Charles's spells).

The glass delusion wasn't unique to Charles VI—it was a recognized, though rare, form of mental illness in the late Middle Ages and Renaissance. But having the King of France suffer from it threw the entire kingdom into turmoil. Charles VI's reign is a tragic story of a monarch battling profound mental illness, leaving behind the unforgettable image of the "Glass King" who feared he might shatter at any moment.

SULTAN IBRAHIM THE MAD:
DROWNING HAREM AND SABLE OBSESSION
(OTTOMAN EMPIRE, MID-17TH C)

The Ottoman Empire had its share of powerful and effective Sultans. Ibrahim I was not one of them. Ruling from 1640 to 1648, his reign was so marked by cruelty, debauchery, and sheer incompetence that he earned the nickname "Ibrahim the Mad." And he lived up to it.

Ibrahim had a rough start. As a potential rival for the throne, he spent most of his youth imprisoned in the "Kafes" (the Cage), a luxurious but isolated part of the palace where princes were kept to prevent them from plotting coups. When his brother Sultan Murad IV died, Ibrahim was suddenly thrust onto the throne, completely unprepared and possibly psychologically damaged by his long confinement.

He quickly developed some... unusual obsessions.

- **Obesity:** He became fixated on extremely overweight women. He sent agents across the empire searching for the fattest women they could find to add to his harem. His favorite consort reportedly weighed around 330 pounds (150 kg).

- **Sable Fur and Ambergris:** He developed an obsession with sable fur (the most expensive fur available) and ambergris (a rare, waxy substance from whales used in perfumes). He demanded his palace be draped in sable, even lining curtains and pillars with it. He taxed heavily to pay for these luxuries.

But his erratic behavior went far beyond strange tastes. He was known for violent mood swings and impulsive cruelty. The most horrifying story involves his entire harem.

According to some accounts (though details are debated by historians), Ibrahim became enraged one day. Why? Maybe he heard a rumor that one of his concubines had been "compromised" by an outsider. Maybe he was just in a paranoid fit. Whatever the trigger, he ordered his chief eunuch to round up **his entire harem**—nearly 300 women—tie them in weighted sacks, and **throw them into the Bosphorus strait to drown.**

Imagine the terror. Hundreds of women, whose only crime was being part of the Sultan's household, allegedly executed on a whim. (One version of the story claims a single concubine survived because her sack wasn't weighted properly and she was rescued by a passing French ship.)

Whether this mass drowning happened exactly as described or is an exaggeration, it reflects the reputation Ibrahim gained for extreme cruelty and unpredictable violence. His spending was out of control, his decisions were erratic, and his focus seemed entirely on personal pleasure and bizarre whims.

Eventually, the ruling elite had enough. The Janissaries (the elite troops), religious leaders, and even his own mother conspired against him. In 1648, Ibrahim was deposed and imprisoned. Ten days later, with the approval of the new Sultan (his young son Mehmed IV) and his mother, Ibrahim the Mad was strangled. His reign was short, chaotic, and left a legacy of madness and brutality.

EMPEROR ELAGABALUS:
TEENAGE TERROR AND SUN GOD
(ROMAN EMPIRE, 218–222 AD)

If you thought Caligula and Nero were bad, wait until you meet Elagabalus. He became Roman Emperor when he was just **14 years old** and managed to cram an astonishing amount of scandal, religious upheaval, and general weirdness into his brief four-year reign (218–222 A.D.).

Elagabalus wasn't his real name (that was Varius Avitus Bassianus). He was the hereditary high priest of the Syrian sun god Elagabal (or Heliogabalus) from the city of Emesa. His powerful grandmother, Julia Maesa (sister of a former empress), cleverly spread a rumor that he was the illegitimate son of the popular previous emperor Caracalla. With army support, she managed to get the teenager proclaimed Emperor of Rome.

Rome wasn't ready for Elagabalus. He arrived in the capital with his Syrian entourage and immediately started shaking things up in the most un-Roman ways possible:

- **Religious Revolution:** He declared his sun god, Elagabal, the chief deity of Rome, placing him *above* Jupiter, the traditional king of the gods. He built a massive temple for Elagabal on Palatine Hill and forced high-ranking senators to participate in bizarre rituals, which reportedly involved dancing around the altar in Syrian priestly robes while drums and cymbals clashed. He even married the sacred Vestal Virgin Aquilia Severa, a shocking act of sacrilege, claiming the marriage between a sun priest and a virgin priestess would produce "godlike children."

- **Scandalous Personal Life:** Roman historians (who were uniformly hostile to him) paint a picture of extreme debauchery. They accused him of cross-dressing, wearing makeup and wigs, offering vast sums to any surgeon who could give him female genitalia, and working as a prostitute out of the imperial palace. He went through five wives and at least one male lover (whom he reportedly called his "husband") in just four years. How much of this is true and how much is slander is hard to say, but his behavior clearly shattered Roman norms.

- **Weird Pranks and Cruelty:** He supposedly enjoyed cruel practical jokes, like releasing venomous snakes into the audience at the gladiatorial games or using a primitive whoopee cushion on his dinner guests. He appointed his lovers and cronies to high office based on whims rather than merit (one story claims he appointed his barber as prefect of the food supply).

Elagabalus seemed determined to offend every traditional Roman value. He replaced respected officials with his Syrian buddies, forced senators to participate in his strange religious ceremonies, and flaunted his unconventional lifestyle.

His grandmother, Julia Maesa, who had put him on the throne, quickly realized she'd made a huge mistake. This kid was uncontrollable and was alienating everyone, especially the powerful

Praetorian Guard (the Emperor's bodyguards). She started promoting Elagabalus's younger, more stable cousin, Alexander Severus, as the heir.

Elagabalus became jealous and tried to have Alexander killed. This was the last straw for the Praetorian Guard. In March 222 A.D., they revolted. Elagabalus (now 18) and his mother were hunted down, murdered, and their bodies dragged through the streets of Rome before being thrown into the Tiber River.

His rule was short, chaotic, and full of scandals—people remembered it as the time a teenage Syrian sun priest tried to force his strange god and weird lifestyle on Rome, which ended as badly as you'd expect.

PETER THE GREAT'S BEARD TAX:
A HAIRY SITUATION (RUSSIA, 1698)

Peter the Great, Tsar of Russia from 1682 to 1725, was a towering figure (literally, he was supposedly 6'8" or 203 cm tall!) who dragged medieval Russia kicking and screaming into the modern world. He built a navy, reformed the army, founded St. Petersburg, and introduced Western European customs. But some of his methods were... forceful. And one of the most famous examples was his war on beards.

In 1697–1698, Peter embarked on a "Grand Embassy," a long tour of Western Europe to learn about new technologies and cultures. He was deeply impressed by the clean-shaven faces, tailored coats, and modern manners he saw in places like Holland and England. He returned to Russia determined to make his own country look less "backward" and more European.

One of the first things he targeted? The long, bushy beards traditionally worn by Russian men, especially the conservative nobles (boyars) and Orthodox priests. In Peter's eyes, these beards were symbols of old-fashioned, Asiatic Russia that he wanted to leave behind.

So, what did he do? He threw a party. A welcome-home reception for his nobles. And then, he pulled out a **barber's razor**.

Imagine the scene: The Tsar himself, the absolute ruler of Russia, personally grabbing his horrified, high-ranking nobles and **shaving off their magnificent beards** on the spot. Resistance was not an option.

This was shocking. In Russian Orthodox tradition, a beard was a symbol of piety and manhood. Shaving it off was seen by many as deeply disrespectful, even sacrilegious.

Peter didn't care. He wanted Russia to be modernized, starting with its faces. He soon put out an order: All men (except priests and peasants) had to shave off their beards.

But Peter was also pragmatic. He knew forcing *everyone* to shave immediately might cause too much unrest. So, he offered a compromise: If you absolutely *insisted* on keeping your beard, you could—but you had to pay a **beard tax**.

The tax varied depending on social status. Wealthy merchants paid a hefty sum (100 rubles a year), court officials and nobles paid less (around 60 rubles), while common townspeople paid a smaller fee. Peasants were largely exempt unless they entered a city.

Anyone who paid the tax received a special **beard token**, usually made of copper or silver. This token served as a receipt, proof that you had paid for the right to keep your facial hair. One side often had an image of a beard and mustache, and the other side read something like "The tax has been taken" or "The beard is a superfluous burden." You had to carry this token with you to avoid being forcibly shaved by officials or guards if you were caught with a beard in public.

The beard tax lasted for decades, long after Peter's initial shaving frenzy. It was deeply unpopular, seen by many as an attack on their traditions and faith. But it was also effective. Over time, clean-shaven faces became the norm among the Russian elite, just as Peter had intended.

It remains a bizarre but telling example of Peter the Great's forceful, top-down approach to modernization—changing his country one shave (or one tax) at a time.

KING PEDRO I:
THE POSTHUMOUS QUEEN OF PORTUGAL (PORTUGAL, 1361)

Love can make people do crazy things. Grief can make them do even crazier things. For King Pedro I of Portugal, love and grief combined to create one of history's most macabre and romantic (in a very twisted way) stories: The time he allegedly exhumed his murdered lover, crowned her corpse Queen, and forced the entire royal court to kiss her decaying hand.

Pedro, while still a prince, was married to Constanza Manuel of Castile for political reasons. But his heart belonged to his wife's lady-in-waiting, the beautiful Inês de Castro. They fell deeply in love and carried on a passionate affair, even having several children together.

This was a huge scandal. Pedro's father, King Afonso IV, and the royal court strongly disapproved. They feared Inês's family would gain too much influence, and that her children might challenge Pedro's legitimate son (from his wife Constanza) for the throne. They tried everything to separate Pedro and Inês—banishment, threats, political maneuvering. Nothing worked. Pedro was devoted to her.

After Pedro's wife Constanza died, he secretly married Inês (or so he later claimed). This only increased the court's alarm. King Afonso IV, convinced Inês was a threat to the stability of the kingdom, made a fateful decision. While Pedro was away on a hunting trip in 1355, Afonso sent three assassins to Inês's monastery retreat. They found her with her children and brutally stabbed her to death.

Pedro was devastated and enraged. He launched a brief civil war against his father. Peace was eventually made, but Pedro never forgave the killers or his father.

Two years later, in 1357, King Afonso IV died, and Pedro finally became King Pedro I of Portugal. Now that he was king, he had the power to get his revenge and honor his lost love in his own seriously weird style.

First, he hunted down two of the three assassins (the third escaped). He didn't just execute them; according to legend, he had their hearts ripped out—one from the chest, one from the back—while they were still alive, declaring they didn't deserve hearts after destroying his.

Then came the truly bizarre part. In 1361, Pedro announced that he *had* secretly married Inês years earlier. Therefore, she was the rightful Queen of Portugal. He ordered her body **exhumed** from its grave.

What happened next is the stuff of gothic legend:

- Inês's decaying corpse was dressed in magnificent royal robes and jewels.

- The corpse was placed on the throne next to Pedro during a grand court ceremony.

- Pedro placed the royal crown upon her skeletal head, declaring her Queen of Portugal.

- He then allegedly **forced every single noble and clergyman in the kingdom** to approach the throne, kneel before the dead queen, and **kiss her decomposing hand** as a sign of allegiance.

Can you imagine the horror? Being forced to pledge loyalty by kissing the hand of a rotting corpse?

After this ghastly coronation, Pedro had two magnificent, matching tombs built at the Monastery of Alcobaça. He had Inês's body interred in one, and gave instructions that when he died, he was to be placed in the other, facing her, so that on Judgment Day, the first thing they would see when they rose would be each other.

Historians debate the literal truth of the coronation ceremony—was it real, or a later embellishment to emphasize Pedro's intense love and grief? But the exhumation, the declaration of her queenship, and the magnificent tombs are historical facts. Pedro I went down in history as "Pedro the Just" or "Pedro the Cruel," but also as the king whose love and grief were so powerful, so all-consuming, that he reached beyond the grave to crown his murdered lover queen in one of history's most unhinged displays of devotion.

MAO ZEDONG OFFERS 10 MILLION WOMEN TO THE USA (CHINA/USA, 1973)

Sometimes, unhinged moments come not from madness, but from awkward attempts at diplomacy (or perhaps very strange humor). This bizarre offer came during a pivotal moment in Cold War history, when the United States and Communist China were cautiously trying to establish relations after decades of hostility.

In February 1973, U.S. Secretary of State Henry Kissinger was visiting Beijing for talks with Chinese leader Mao Zedong. Mao was the top leader of China, an old revolutionary famous for his big statements and sometimes rough, unpredictable way of doing things.

During a late-night meeting in Mao's private residence, the conversation turned to trade and the perceived lack of it between the two giant nations. Kissinger mentioned the potential for the US to sell technology to China.

Then, according to the official U.S. transcript released decades later, Mao suddenly changed the subject. Complaining about China having "too many women," he made an astonishing offer.

Mao: "You know China is a very poor country... We don't have much. What we have in excess is women. So if you want them we can give a few of those to you. Some tens of thousands."

Kissinger, likely taken aback but trying to play along, joked, "We have no quota."

Mao: "We can let them come to your place. They will create disasters. That way you can lessen our burdens." He then laughed.

Kissinger, perhaps unsure if Mao was serious, tried to steer the conversation back to trade, mentioning Soviet threats. But Mao wasn't done.

Mao: "Let them go to your place. They will create disasters. That way you can lessen our burdens... Do you want our Chinese women? We can give you ten million."

Kissinger, trying to deflect with humor, replied, "The Chairman is improving his offer."

Mao: "We have too many women... They give birth to children and our children are too many."

Kissinger diplomatically tried to change the subject again, saying, "We will study the problem."

Later, a female Chinese diplomat present at the meeting reportedly told Kissinger that Mao's comments were inappropriate and asked that they be struck from the official record, fearing they would be misinterpreted. Kissinger agreed.

What was Mao thinking? Was it a serious, albeit clumsy, attempt to highlight China's population issues? Was it a bizarre attempt at humor? Was it a way to shock the Americans or test their reactions? Was it a sign that the old leader's mind was starting to slip?

Probably a mix of things. Mao was known for making provocative statements. Offering millions of women as an export commodity, however, was definitely out there, even for him. It was a moment of unhinged diplomacy, a strange footnote in the complex process of opening relations between two superpowers, leaving American diplomats wondering if they'd heard correctly. "Did he really just offer us ten million women?"

POPE ALEXANDER VI (BORGIA):
RENAISSANCE SCANDAL KING (ROME, 1492–1503)

The Renaissance Papacy wasn't always known for its piety, but Pope Alexander VI, born Rodrigo Borgia, took corruption, nepotism, and scandal to a whole new level. His reign (1492–1503) is infamous for its ruthless ambition, blatant favoritism toward his own children, and rumors of debauchery that shocked even Renaissance Italy. If any Pope seemed to be "losing it" in terms of moral compass, it was Alexander VI.

First off, how did he become Pope? Through **bribery**, plain and simple. The papal election (conclave) of 1492 was notoriously corrupt, with Rodrigo Borgia, already a wealthy and powerful Cardinal, allegedly buying votes with promises of offices, land, and cold, hard cash. He basically bought the Papacy.

Once he became Pope, his main goal seemed to be making his own family more powerful and rich, especially his illegitimate children (who he admitted were his, which was scandalous for a Pope).

- **Cesare Borgia:** His ruthless and ambitious son was made a Cardinal at age 18 (despite having little interest in religion), then later renounced the cardinalate to become a military commander, carving out a territory for himself in central Italy with his father's papal armies and funds. Cesare became the model for Machiavelli's "The Prince"—a symbol of cunning, ruthless politics.

- **Lucrezia Borgia:** His daughter was used as a political pawn, married off three times to forge alliances. Rumors (likely exaggerated by enemies) swirled around her, accusing her of incest with her father and brother, and of being a poisoner. While probably untrue, the rumors reflect the scandalous reputation of the family.

Alexander VI himself lived more like a secular prince than a spiritual leader. The Vatican under his rule was known for lavish banquets, parties, and rumors of orgies. One notorious event, the "Banquet of the Chestnuts," reported by a contemporary diarist (though possibly exaggerated), allegedly involved 50 prostitutes entertaining cardinals and papal staff with lewd performances.

He used papal power ruthlessly, waging wars, forming alliances, breaking treaties, and excommunicating enemies to further his family's ambitions. He sold church offices (simony) on a massive scale to raise money. Critics who spoke out against him, like the fiery preacher Girolamo Savonarola in Florence, were often excommunicated, arrested, tortured, and executed.

Was Alexander VI clinically "mad"? Probably not in the sense of Charles VI or Ibrahim. But was he morally unhinged, completely losing sight of the supposed spiritual mission of the Papacy in his lust for power and family advancement? Absolutely. His reign is often seen as the low point of the Renaissance Papacy, a time when corruption and worldly ambition seemed to completely eclipse religious duty. He ruled like a king, not a pope, leaving behind a legacy of scandal that still fascinates and repels historians today.

IVAN THE TERRIBLE: RUSSIA'S REIGN OF TERROR (RUSSIA, 16TH C)

The first Russian ruler to officially take the title "Tsar" (Caesar), Ivan IV Vasilyevich (reigned 1547–1584) started promisingly but descended into paranoia, cruelty, and fits of rage that earned him the chilling nickname "Ivan the Terrible" (or more accurately translated from Russian, "Ivan the Fearsome" or "Ivan the Awe-Inspiring," but "Terrible" stuck).

Ivan's childhood was brutal. His father died when he was three, his mother was likely poisoned when he was eight, and he grew up in a court filled with scheming, power-hungry nobles (boyars) who ignored or abused him. This likely contributed to his lifelong suspicion and ruthlessness.

Early in his reign, he was actually quite effective—he reformed the government, created a new legal code, and conquered significant territory. But after the death of his beloved first wife, Anastasia, in 1560 (whom he suspected the boyars had poisoned), Ivan's behavior became increasingly erratic and violent.

His descent into "losing it" culminated in several key actions:

- **The Oprichnina (1565–1572):** Convinced the boyars were plotting against him, Ivan created his own private territory within Russia called the Oprichnina, ruled directly by him and policed by his terrifying personal guard, the **Oprichniki**. These black-clad horsemen rode black horses, carried severed dog heads and brooms on their saddles (symbolizing sniffing out treason and sweeping it away), and unleashed a reign of terror. They arrested, tortured, exiled, and executed thousands of people Ivan suspected of disloyalty, seizing their lands and spreading fear throughout Russia. It was basically a state-sponsored terrorist organization run by the Tsar himself.

- **The Massacre of Novgorod (1570):** Suspecting the entire city of Novgorod of plotting to defect to rival Poland-Lithuania, Ivan led his Oprichniki on a brutal campaign. For several weeks, the city was systematically sacked. Thousands of citizens—men, women, and children—were tortured and killed in horrific ways. Churches were looted; homes destroyed. Estimates of the dead range from a few thousand to tens of thousands. He was punishing a whole group of people in a way that's almost too horrifying to imagine.

- **Killing His Son (1581):** In a fit of uncontrollable rage, Ivan struck his eldest son and heir, also named Ivan, with his pointed staff during an argument (possibly over his son's wife or military matters). The blow proved fatal. Ivan was immediately consumed with grief and remorse, reportedly howling in anguish and clinging to his son's body, but it was too late. He had killed his own successor in a moment of fury.

Ivan's reign swung wildly between periods of capable leadership and terrifying bouts of paranoia and violence. He was deeply religious yet capable of appalling cruelty. He expanded Russia's territory but also terrorized its people. His "terribleness" wasn't just about being fearsome; it was about the unpredictable, unhinged violence of a ruler consumed by suspicion and rage.

JUANA THE MAD:
LOVE, GRIEF, AND A TRAVELING CORPSE
(SPAIN, EARLY 16TH C)

History remembers her as "Juana la Loca"—Juana the Mad. Was she really insane, or just a victim of bad luck, overwhelming sadness, and the political scheming of the men in her life? Probably a bit of both. But her story, particularly her obsessive devotion to her dead husband, is undeniably unhinged.

Juana was the daughter of the famous Ferdinand II of Aragon and Isabella I of Castile—the Spanish monarchs who funded Christopher Columbus. She was married off young to Philip the Handsome, Duke of Burgundy, heir to the Habsburg lands. By all accounts, Juana fell deeply, passionately, and obsessively in love with her husband. Philip, however, was known for his good looks and wandering eye, and his frequent infidelities reportedly drove Juana into fits of jealous rage. Stories circulated of her attacking his supposed mistresses.

Despite the turbulent relationship, Juana inherited the throne of Castile after her mother's death in 1504. Her father, Ferdinand, and her husband, Philip, immediately started vying for control, both claiming Juana was mentally unstable and unfit to rule.

Then, in 1506, Philip the Handsome died suddenly (possibly from typhoid fever) at the age of 28. Juana's already fragile mental state completely shattered. Her grief was all-consuming.

This is where things get really weird:

- **Refusal to Bury Him:** Juana refused to allow Philip's body to be buried immediately. She kept his coffin with her, occasionally opening it to gaze upon his embalmed face, kiss his feet, or talk to him.

- **The Funeral Procession From Hell:** She decided to transport Philip's body from Burgos, where he died, south to Granada, the royal burial place chosen by her parents. This journey took **eight months**. Juana traveled only at night, supposedly because "a widow who had lost the sun of her own soul should not travel in the light of day." She ordered that no women were allowed near the coffin, fearing even in death Philip might be tempted by them. The procession would stop at monasteries along the way, with the coffin placed near Juana's chambers.

- **Years of Vigil:** Even after finally reaching Granada, Juana didn't bury Philip right away. She kept his coffin at a convent near her residence for years, reportedly visiting it frequently.

Meanwhile, her father Ferdinand took control of Castile as regent, keeping Juana largely confined. After Ferdinand's death, Juana's own son, Charles (later Holy Roman Emperor Charles V), arrived in Spain. He, too, deemed his mother unfit to rule.

In 1509, Charles had Juana permanently confined to the Royal Convent of Santa Clara in Tordesillas. She remained imprisoned there for the rest of her life—**nearly 50 years**—separated from most of her children and stripped of any real power. Philip's coffin remained nearby for much of that time.

Was Juana truly "mad"? She certainly exhibited signs of severe depression, anxiety, and obsessive behavior, likely exacerbated by her intense grief and the political betrayals she suffered. But her "madness" was also conveniently used by her father and son to usurp her power. Regardless of the diagnosis, her story is a tragic tale of love, loss, and a grief so profound it led her to travel across Spain with her husband's corpse in tow, earning her the unforgettable title Juana the Mad.

EMPEROR ZHENGDE:
THE IMPERIAL PRANKSTER (CHINA, EARLY 16TH C)

Being Emperor of China came with immense power and responsibility. Emperor Zhengde (reigned 1505–1521) of the Ming Dynasty, however, seemed more interested in goofing off, playing elaborate games, and generally avoiding his imperial duties. He wasn't necessarily "mad" in a violent or paranoid way, but his behavior was so childish, irresponsible, and bizarre that his officials constantly despaired, marking him as one of China's most unhinged rulers in terms of sheer neglect and absurdity.

Zhengde became emperor as a teenager and was quickly influenced by powerful eunuchs who pushed him to have fun instead of actually governing. He seemed utterly bored by the tedious rituals and responsibilities of ruling. His escapades included:

- **The Imaginary Alter Ego:** Zhengde created an alter ego for himself named **Zhu Shou**, supposedly a brave military general. He would issue orders to himself *as Zhu Shou*, promote Zhu Shou through the ranks, and even send messages back and forth between "Emperor Zhengde" and "General Zhu Shou." He would leave the palace in disguise, pretending to be Zhu Shou, and participate in military expeditions (often turning them into chaotic sightseeing tours).

- **Building a Fake City:** He disliked the formality of the Forbidden City (the imperial palace complex in Beijing). So, adjacent to it, he built a replica palace district called the "Leopard Quarter." This wasn't just extra living space; it was basically his personal playground, filled with houses, shops, temples, and streets, staffed by eunuchs and soldiers dressed up as merchants, innkeepers, and performers. He would roam this fake city in disguise, pretending to be a commoner, haggling in shops, visiting mock brothels, and generally playing make-believe.

- **Obsession With Foreign Languages and Lamas:** He became fascinated with foreign languages like Tibetan, Sanskrit, and Arabic, forcing his officials to learn them too. He also developed a deep interest in Tibetan Buddhism, inviting many lamas (monks) to court, showering them with gifts, and participating in their rituals—much to the dismay of his Confucian-trained officials.

- **Dangerous Pranks and Accidents:** His love for excitement often bordered on reckless. He enjoyed handling explosives and artillery, leading to accidents where palace buildings caught fire. He loved hunting and military games, sometimes putting himself and others in danger. During one trip on the Grand Canal, he fell off his boat while drunk and nearly drowned; he contracted an illness from the incident and died a few months later at the age of 29.

- **Neglecting Duties:** While the Emperor played general or pretended to be a shopkeeper, urgent government business piled up. Officials struggled to get his attention, memorials went unread, and important decisions were left to corrupt eunuchs. His reign saw rising corruption and instability.

Emperor Zhengde wasn't necessarily cruel or tyrannical like some other rulers on this list. He was more like a spoiled, hyperactive kid given the keys to an empire. His refusal to take his role seriously, his elaborate fantasies, and his pursuit of personal amusement over governing make his reign a prime example of imperial irresponsibility and a uniquely unhinged chapter in Chinese history. He wasn't losing his mind; he just seemed determined not to use it for its intended purpose.

PART 3:

ANIMAL CHAOS:
WHEN BEASTS MADE HISTORY

Humans like to think they run the show. We build cities, write laws, fight wars, and generally act like we're the main characters on Planet Earth. But sometimes? Sometimes, the animal kingdom crashes the party. And when animals get involved in human history, things tend to get weird, chaotic, and hilariously unpredictable.

Get ready for the furry, feathered, and sometimes slimy side of unhinged history. This section is all about those moments when animals took center stage, often with disastrous or just plain bizarre results.

We're talking about military experiments involving camels in the American desert (spoiler: didn't go well), Napoleon Bonaparte getting punked by bunnies, bears that officially joined the army, whales that exploded (messily), and chickens that supposedly predicted the end of the world. We'll even meet animals put on trial for crimes and monkeys mistaken for enemy spies.

From diplomatic giraffes to weaponized pigeons, history is full of tales where beasts, big and small, threw a wrench into human plans or became unlikely historical figures themselves. So, let's dive into the animal chaos and see what happens when human history meets the wild kingdom.

The Great American Camel Fail (USA, 1850s)

The American Southwest in the mid-19th century was vast, dry, and rugged territory. Getting supplies and soldiers across these dry lands was a huge headache for the U.S. Army. Horses and mules struggled with the heat and lack of water. So, someone in the War Department had a brilliant, if slightly bizarre, idea: **Camels!**

The logic seemed sound. Camels are perfectly adapted to desert environments. They can carry heavy loads, go for days without water, and eat tough desert plants that would kill a horse. If they worked in the deserts of Africa and the Middle East, why not Arizona and Texas?

In 1855, Congress approved $30,000 (a hefty sum then) for the "purchase and importation of camels and dromedaries to be employed for military purposes." An army officer was dispatched to the Mediterranean and the Middle East. He returned with over 70 camels of various types and several experienced camel drivers, including a Syrian man nicknamed "Hi Jolly" (Hadji Ali).

The **U.S. Army Camel Corps** was born.

Initially, the camels performed amazingly well. They easily carried heavier loads than mules, traveled faster across rough terrain, needed far less water, and seemed unfazed by the desert heat. During survey expeditions, they proved their worth, outperforming traditional pack animals. Success! Right?

Wrong. There was one major problem the planners hadn't fully considered: **Camels are not horses.** And American soldiers were horse people.

- **They Smelled Bad:** Soldiers complained constantly about the camels' strong odor.

- **They Were Grumpy:** Camels can be notoriously ill-tempered. They spit, bite, and kick. The soldiers didn't know how to handle them, and the camels didn't appreciate being mishandled.

- **They Spooked the Horses:** Horses and mules were terrified of the strange-looking, strange-smelling camels, often panicking and bolting when they encountered them. This caused chaos on joint expeditions.

- **Their Feet Weren't Right:** While great on sand, camel feet sometimes struggled on the rocky terrain common in parts of the American Southwest.

- **Cultural Clash:** The American soldiers just didn't like or trust the camels. They were unfamiliar, difficult, and just plain *weird*. The experienced Middle Eastern handlers often clashed with the army personnel.

Even though the camels were physically better suited for the job, the people involved messed things up. When the American Civil War broke out in 1861, the Camel Corps experiment was largely abandoned. The camels were auctioned off, sold to circuses, used by miners, or simply turned loose into the desert.

For decades afterwards, sightings of feral camels roaming the deserts of Arizona and Texas occasionally startled prospectors and travelers. Hi Jolly, the Syrian camel driver, stayed in Arizona, becoming a local legend.

The U.S. Army Camel Corps remains a curious footnote in military history—a perfectly logical idea on paper that failed completely because, sometimes, you just can't convince horse people to become camel people.

NAPOLEON VS. THE BUNNIES: ATTACK OF THE KILLER RABBITS (FRANCE, 1807)

Napoleon Bonaparte. Emperor of the French. Military genius. Conqueror of Europe. Master strategist. Man who was once forced into a panicked retreat by... a horde of fluffy bunnies.

Yes, you read that right.

The story takes place in 1807, at the height of Napoleon's power. He had just signed the Treaties of Tilsit, ending the war between France and Imperial Russia. To celebrate this momentous occasion, Napoleon suggested a rabbit hunt. A grand imperial rabbit hunt!

His chief of staff, Alexandre Berthier, was tasked with organizing the event. Berthier wanted to impress the Emperor, so he didn't skimp. He reportedly got his hands on hundreds, maybe even thousands, of rabbits from local farmers. These weren't wild rabbits; they were domesticated bunnies, raised in cages. Berthier had them released into a large field where Napoleon and his distinguished guests could enjoy a leisurely day of shooting.

The hunters took their positions. The cages were opened. The rabbits were released.

And then, things went wrong. Hilariously wrong.

These weren't frightened wild rabbits scattering in all directions. These were tame rabbits who associated humans with food. Instead of running *away* from Napoleon and his hunting party, the massive swarm of bunnies saw the most powerful man in Europe and thought, "Lunchtime!"

They charged.

Hundreds, possibly thousands, of fluffy rabbits bounded *toward* Napoleon. They swarmed around his legs, reportedly trying to climb up his imperial jacket. Napoleon, initially amused, soon found himself completely besieged by a relentless tide of hungry bunnies.

His hunting party tried to shoo them away with riding crops and sticks. Napoleon himself reportedly tried batting at them. Nothing worked. The rabbits were relentless, a fuzzy wave overwhelming the conqueror of Europe.

According to the stories, Napoleon, the guy who led huge armies, was forced to beat a hasty retreat. He scrambled back toward his carriage, still pursued by the most aggressive elements of the rabbit army, some supposedly even dividing into flanking groups. He leaped into the safety of his coach, and the bunnies were eventually driven off.

Imagine the scene: The Emperor of France, fresh off diplomatic triumphs, fleeing in disarray from a swarm of cuddly rabbits. Berthier was undoubtedly mortified. Napoleon was probably less than amused.

It's a small, absurd incident, but a wonderful reminder that even the most powerful figures in history aren't immune to moments of utter chaos, especially when hungry bunnies are involved.

WHEN WHALES EXPLODE:
OREGON'S BLUBBER BLUNDER (USA, 1970)

Sometimes, the "animal chaos" happens after the animal is already dead. Case in point: the infamous exploding whale of Florence, Oregon.

In November 1970, a massive 45-foot, eight-ton sperm whale washed ashore on the Oregon coast. This presented a problem: how to get rid of a giant, decaying whale carcass? Leaving it to rot would create an unbearable stench for beachgoers and nearby residents. Burying it seemed impossible due to its size and the sandy location. They decided that cutting it up and hauling it away would be too difficult.

The Oregon Highway Division (now ODOT), for reasons that remain baffling, was put in charge. Engineer George Thornton came up with a plan that seemed logical, if you squinted really hard and ignored common sense: **Blow it up.**

The idea was that a controlled dynamite explosion would disintegrate the whale into small, bite-sized pieces. The blast would scatter these pieces harmlessly into the ocean, or maybe seagulls and crabs would clean them up. What could possibly go wrong?

Thornton consulted with military explosives experts (who apparently weren't consulted *enough*) and decided that half a ton (about 20 cases) of dynamite should do the trick.

On November 12, 1970, a crowd gathered at a safe distance. A local news crew, KATU reporter Paul Linnman and cameraman Doug Brazil, were there to film the event. Thornton gave the signal.

KABOOM!

The explosion was spectacular. But it didn't quite go according to plan. Instead of disintegrating the whale into seagull snacks, the blast sent massive chunks of rotting whale blubber flying high into the air and, crucially, back toward the land.

Huge pieces of blubber rained down on the horrified spectators and the surrounding area. One enormous chunk, described as the size of a coffee table, landed on and completely crushed the roof of a nearby car (luckily, no one was inside). Smaller pieces splattered everywhere, coating people and property in rancid whale goo.

And the main part of the whale carcass? It barely moved. The explosion had mostly just carved a large crater underneath it. The problem hadn't been solved; it had just been made much, much messier.

The KATU news report, featuring Linnman's deadpan commentary over footage of flying blubber and the crushed car, became an instant classic of unintentional comedy and government incompetence. ("The blast blasted blubber beyond all believable bounds," Linnman famously reported).

In the end, highway crews had to resort to the method they'd initially dismissed: manually cutting up the remaining carcass and burying the pieces.

The Oregon exploding whale incident remains a legendary example of a plan backfiring in the most spectacular and disgusting way possible, a testament to the fact that sometimes, nature (even dead nature) refuses to cooperate with dynamite.

Guilty as Charged:
The Pig That Was Hanged for Murder (France, 1386)

Think courtrooms are just for humans? Think again. Throughout the Middle Ages and the Renaissance in Europe, there was a bizarre legal practice known as **animal trials**. Animals—from pigs and dogs to rats and even insects like weevils—could be formally charged with crimes, brought before a court (sometimes secular, sometimes religious), assigned lawyers, tried, and, if found guilty, sentenced.

The sentences could range from exile or excommunication (for pests like rats or locusts, often tried by church courts) to imprisonment or even execution for larger animals accused of harming humans or property.

One of the most famous and well-documented cases occurred in Falaise, Normandy, France, in 1386. The defendant? **A pig.**

The charge? **Murder.**

According to court records, the pig had attacked the infant child of a local mason, horribly mutilating the baby's face and arm. The injuries were so severe that the child died soon after.

The pig was arrested and imprisoned in the local jail, just like a human suspect. A formal trial was convened. The pig was brought before the court. Evidence was presented. Witnesses likely testified. We don't know if the pig had a lawyer (sometimes animals did, assigned by the court to argue why things weren't so bad), but the result was grim.

The pig was found **guilty** of murder.

The sentence? **Death by hanging.**

But the punishment didn't stop there. In a truly bizarre twist reflecting the idea of making the punishment fit the crime, the pig was first dressed in **human clothing**—specifically, a waistcoat, gloves, and drawers. Then, mimicking the injuries it had inflicted on the child, the pig was reportedly mutilated on its head and forelegs. Finally, the dressed-up, wounded pig was taken to the public square and hanged from a gibbet until dead.

The execution was a public spectacle, meant to serve as a warning and uphold justice. The town even paid for the pig's human clothes and the executioner's services, and the costs were meticulously recorded in the town's accounts.

Why did people put animals on trial? Historians have various theories. Maybe it was a way to restore social order after a shocking event. Maybe it showed they believed animals knew right from wrong and could be blamed for what they did. Maybe it was a way to understand and control chaotic natural events within a legal framework. Maybe it was just plain weird.

Whatever the reason, the image of a pig in a waistcoat and gloves being hanged for murder is a stark reminder of a time when the lines between human and animal justice were disturbingly, unhingedly blurred.

Wojtek the Soldier Bear:
Private Bear of the Polish Army (WWII)

Some soldiers carry rifles, some carry ammo, and some... carry artillery shells and drink beer with their comrades. Meet Wojtek, the Syrian brown bear who became an officially enlisted soldier in the Polish Army during World War II.

Wojtek's story begins in 1942 in Iran. A group of Polish soldiers, recently released from Soviet captivity and making their way to join the Allied forces, encountered a young Iranian boy who had found an orphaned bear cub. The soldiers bought the cub, named him Wojtek (meaning "Smiling Warrior" or "He Who Enjoys War"), and adopted him as their unofficial mascot.

Wojtek quickly became the beloved pet of the 22nd Artillery Supply Company. He grew up among the soldiers, mimicking their behavior. He learned to salute, enjoyed wrestling with the troops (usually winning), and developed a taste for beer (which he'd drink straight from the bottle) and cigarettes (which he'd eat rather than smoke). He slept in tents with the men or in a custom wooden crate.

As the Polish forces moved through Iraq, Syria, Palestine, and Egypt, Wojtek went with them. He became a huge morale booster, a furry friend in the midst of war. But when it was time for the Polish II Corps to go to Italy and fight with the British 8th Army, there was a hitch: Rules didn't allow mascot animals on British transport ships.

The Polish soldiers came up with a brilliant solution: They couldn't take a pet bear, but they *could* take a fellow soldier. They **officially enlisted Wojtek into the Polish Army**. He was given the rank of Private, assigned a serial number, and listed on the company roster. Private Wojtek was now, technically, a soldier.

He sailed with his unit to Italy. During the fierce Battle of Monte Cassino in 1944, one of the toughest battles on the Italian front, Wojtek truly earned his stripes. His company was responsible for transporting heavy crates of artillery ammunition to the front lines under fire. Seeing his human comrades struggling with the heavy boxes, Wojtek apparently decided to help.

He stood on his hind legs, approached the trucks, and held out his paws. The soldiers, astonished, gave him a crate. Wojtek effortlessly carried the 100-pound (45 kg) crate of mortar shells, stacking it with the others. He kept doing this through the whole battle, never dropping a crate, calmly carrying essential ammo while shells exploded nearby.

His bravery and usefulness were undeniable. In recognition of his service, the 22nd Company adopted a new emblem: A silhouette of a bear carrying an artillery shell.

After the war, with Poland falling under communist control, the 22nd Company was demobilized in Scotland in 1947. Wojtek couldn't go back to Poland with them. He was honorably discharged and spent the rest of his life at the Edinburgh Zoo, where he was a popular attraction, often visited by his former Polish comrades who would sometimes jump into his enclosure to wrestle with him or toss him cigarettes (which the zookeepers discouraged).

Wojtek died in 1963. He remains a beloved figure in Poland and Scotland, a unique example of animal companionship and bravery in wartime—the beer-drinking, cigarette-eating bear who became an official soldier and helped fight the Nazis.

MRS. O'LEARY'S COW:
THE SCAPEGOAT OF THE GREAT CHICAGO FIRE (USA, 1871)

Did a clumsy cow kicking over a lantern really start the Great Chicago Fire of 1871, one of the most devastating fires in American history? Probably not. But the story stuck, turning poor Mrs. O'Leary's bovine into the most famous (and unfairly blamed) animal arsonist of all time.

The Great Chicago Fire raged from October 8th to 10th, 1871. It killed around 300 people, left 100,000 homeless, and destroyed over three square miles of the city. Chicago at the time was built largely of wood, had suffered a dry summer, and strong winds fanned the flames, creating a terrifying firestorm.

The fire definitely started in or near the barn behind the cottage of Patrick and Catherine O'Leary at 137 DeKoven Street. The O'Learys were poor Irish immigrants. So, how did the cow get involved?

Almost immediately after the fire, newspapers started printing the story: Catherine O'Leary had been milking her cow late at night in the barn. The cow, startled or just clumsy, kicked over the kerosene lantern she was using, igniting the hay and starting the blaze that consumed the city.

This story spread like... well, wildfire. It was simple, dramatic, and provided an easy explanation for the catastrophe. It also tapped into anti-immigrant prejudice prevalent at the time—blaming the disaster on a poor Irish family felt convenient for some. Michael Ahern, a reporter for the *Chicago Republican*, later admitted he and colleagues might have fabricated the cow story to make colorful copy.

Catherine O'Leary herself vehemently denied it. She swore she was in bed when the fire started and didn't milk her cows late at night. Neighbors corroborated her account. The official inquiry into the fire concluded that the cause was unknown, though it did confirm the fire started near the O'Leary barn. Theories ranged from careless smokers, sparks from a chimney, or even spontaneous combustion in the hayloft.

Despite the lack of evidence, the image of Mrs. O'Leary's cow kicking over the lantern became indelibly linked with the Great Chicago Fire. It appeared in illustrations, songs, poems, and popular history for decades. Mrs. O'Leary became a recluse, harassed and blamed for the disaster until her death in 1895.

Finally, in 1997, the Chicago City Council officially exonerated Catherine O'Leary and her cow, passing a resolution that declared the evidence against them was flimsy and blaming the reporter who likely invented the story.

So, while the O'Leary cow probably didn't start the fire, she remains a powerful symbol of how easily blame can be assigned in times of chaos, and how a convenient story—especially one involving animal chaos—can take on a life of its own, even if it means scapegoating an innocent immigrant family and their unfortunate cow.

HANNIBAL'S SNAKE BOMBS:
REPTILIAN NAVAL WARFARE
(ANCIENT ROME VS. BITHYNIA, ~184 B.C.)

Hannibal Barca, the Carthaginian general famous for marching elephants over the Alps to attack Rome, was one of history's most brilliant and unconventional military minds. He wasn't afraid to think outside the box—or, in this case, outside the clay pot filled with venomous snakes.

Long after his famous campaigns against Rome in the Second Punic War, Hannibal found himself in exile, serving King Prusias I of Bithynia (a kingdom in modern-day Turkey). Bithynia was at war with a rival kingdom, Pergamum, which was allied with Rome and led by King Eumenes II. Eumenes had a much larger and more powerful navy than Prusias. Hannibal, serving as Prusias's advisor and naval commander, needed a clever trick to even the odds.

His solution? Biological warfare, ancient-world style. **Snake bombs.**

Hannibal ordered his sailors to gather as many **venomous snakes** as they could find. They packed these angry reptiles into earthenware pots. Before a major naval battle against the Pergamene fleet (around 184 B.C.), Hannibal gave his sailors specific instructions. He told them to ignore most of the enemy ships and concentrate all their efforts on attacking one specific vessel: King Eumenes's flagship.

How would they identify it? Hannibal had sent messengers (heralds) in a boat *before* the battle, carrying a sealed message supposedly for Eumenes. This wasn't a peace offer; it was a clever ruse to identify the king's ship for his snake-pot crews.

As the battle began, the Bithynian sailors did what they were told. They rowed hard toward the identified flagship. As they got close, they didn't try to ram or board it. Instead, they started **hurling the clay pots full of venomous snakes** onto the deck of Eumenes's ship.

Imagine the chaos. Suddenly, the deck of the flagship is swarming with angry, poisonous snakes slithering out of shattered pots. The Pergamene sailors, who were expecting swords and spears, were completely unprepared for this reptilian assault. Panic erupted. Sailors likely abandoned their posts, trying desperately to avoid being bitten. Fighting effectively became impossible amidst the snake infestation.

While Eumenes's flagship descended into chaos, the rest of the Pergamene fleet was initially confused. Why were the Bithynians ignoring them and just throwing pots at their king? By the time they realized what was happening, the damage was done. Eumenes managed to escape, but his command structure was disrupted, and the Bithynians, despite being outnumbered, were able to win the naval battle thanks to Hannibal's slithery strategy.

It was a brilliant, terrifying, and utterly unhinged tactic—using pots full of snakes as naval projectiles. Only a mind like Hannibal's could come up with something so bizarrely effective.

THE WHALE THAT FOUGHT BACK:
SINKING THE ESSEX (PACIFIC OCEAN, 1820)

Whales were big business in the early 19th century. Whale oil lit lamps and lubricated machinery, making whaling ships hunt these giants across the globe. It was dangerous work, but usually, the danger came from storms, accidents, or the sheer difficulty of harpooning and processing a massive creature. Rarely did the whale itself turn the tables so dramatically as the one that attacked the Nantucket whaleship *Essex* in 1820.

The *Essex*, captained by George Pollard Jr., was on a long whaling voyage in the remote South Pacific, thousands of miles from the coast of South America. On November 20, 1820, the lookout spotted whales. Three small whaleboats were launched, manned by harpooners and oarsmen, including First Mate Owen Chase and cabin boy Thomas Nickerson.

While two boats successfully harpooned whales, Chase's boat was damaged when a whale smacked it with its tail, forcing him to return to the *Essex* for repairs. As they worked on deck, a truly enormous sperm whale, estimated at 85 feet long (much larger than typical males), appeared near the ship.

At first, it lay motionless. Then, it charged.

The massive whale rammed the *Essex* head-on, shaking the entire vessel. It swam off, turned, and charged *again*, this time hitting the bow with even greater force, shattering timbers and causing the ship to rapidly take on water.

The crew, stunned and terrified, barely had time to gather basic supplies (hardtack biscuits, water, navigation tools) before the 238-ton whaleship capsized and began to sink in the middle of the vast Pacific Ocean. The men scrambled into the three small, leaky whaleboats.

Twenty men were now floating aimlessly, thousands of miles from land, with hardly any food or water. What followed was one of the most harrowing survival ordeals in maritime history. They faced starvation, dehydration, scorching sun, storms, sharks, and madness. They resorted to cannibalism to survive.

At first, they tried sailing to South America, but fearing cannibals on nearby islands (ironically), they started a much longer, dangerous trip instead. After 93 days at sea, only eight of the original twenty men survived to be rescued, found in two separate boats, emaciated and traumatized. Captain Pollard and another man survived in one boat; Owen Chase, Thomas Nickerson, and another survivor were in a second boat. A third boat disappeared entirely.

First Mate Owen Chase later wrote a harrowing account of the disaster, *Narrative of the Most Extraordinary and Distressing Shipwreck of the Whale-Ship Essex*. This incredible true story of a whale deliberately attacking and sinking a ship, and the horrific survival tale that followed, directly inspired Herman Melville to write his masterpiece, **Moby Dick.**

The *Essex* disaster was a terrifying reminder of the power of nature and the dangers faced by whalers. It was a rare, shocking instance where the hunted turned hunter, a whale seemingly taking revenge and creating a legend that would echo through literature forever.

THE PROPHET HEN OF LEEDS: APOCALYPSE EGGS (ENGLAND, 1806)

People have always looked for signs and warnings, especially about the world ending. In 1806, in the town of Leeds, England, it seemed the apocalypse warnings were coming from a very unusual source: **a chicken.**

A local hen, owned by a woman named Mary Bateman, suddenly started laying eggs inscribed with a chilling message: **"Christ is coming."**

News of the miracle eggs spread like wildfire. Leeds was gripped by excitement and fear. People flocked to Mary Bateman's house to see the prophetic poultry and her miraculous eggs. Many were convinced it was a divine sign, a warning that the Day of Judgment was imminent. They prayed, they repented, they paid Mary Bateman pennies to witness the miracle firsthand. Mary, previously poor, started doing quite well from her prophetic hen.

Skeptics existed, of course, but the phenomenon continued. More eggs appeared bearing the ominous message. The crowds grew larger. Was this humble hen truly a messenger from God?

A suspicious local decided to investigate. He hid himself near Mary Bateman's house one night and watched. What he saw wasn't divine intervention, but human trickery. He caught Mary Bateman in the act!

Her method was simple but devious. She would write the message "Christ is coming" on an egg using corrosive ink (likely vinegar or acid). Then, she would carefully **reinsert the doctored egg back into the poor hen's oviduct.** Later, when the hen naturally laid the egg (again), voila! A miracle message appeared!

The hoax was exposed. The crowds turned angry. Mary Bateman, far from being the owner of a prophet hen, was revealed as a clever fraudster (and she later turned out to be involved in far worse crimes, including theft, fraud, and possibly even murder, eventually being hanged for poisoning in 1809).

The Prophet Hen of Leeds remains a bizarre example of public gullibility and hoaxing. It shows how easily people can be swayed by supposed miracles, especially during uncertain times, and how even a humble chicken could briefly become the center of apocalyptic frenzy thanks to a bit of acid ink and some uncomfortable poultry manipulation.

GIRAFFE DIPLOMACY:
THE ANIMAL THAT DAZZLED EUROPE
(EGYPT/FRANCE, 1826–1827)

Sometimes, animal chaos isn't about destruction, but about causing a sensation. In the 1820s, a single giraffe sent as a diplomatic gift from Egypt to France caused a level of public excitement and obsession never seen before, becoming arguably the most famous animal in Europe.

The giraffe, a young female, was a gift from Muhammad Ali Pasha, the Ottoman Viceroy of Egypt, to King Charles X of France. Why? Diplomacy. Muhammad Ali wanted France's help against the Ottoman Sultan, and a spectacular, exotic gift seemed like a good way to get on their good side. He actually sent two giraffes—one to France, and one to Great Britain (the British one died relatively quickly). The French one, however, became a superstar.

She arrived in Marseille in late 1826 after a long sea voyage. But how to get her from the port city of Marseille all the way to the King in Paris? Walking seemed the only option.

So began an epic **550-mile (880 km) journey on foot** across France in the spring of 1827. The young giraffe, accompanied by her Egyptian keepers, several cows (to provide her milk), and a procession of scientists and guards led by naturalist Étienne Geoffroy Saint-Hilaire, walked north.

This had never happened before. Most French people had never even *seen* a giraffe, let alone had one walking through their town square. The journey became a national event. Crowds lined the route in every town and village, cheering and marveling at the strange, long-necked creature. It was like a royal procession, but with a giraffe. She was given special boots to protect her feet and a custom two-part coat to keep her warm.

By the time she reached Paris after a six-week walk, **"la girafe"** was the biggest celebrity in the country. Her arrival caused absolute pandemonium. An estimated 100,000 people (about one-eighth of Paris's population) turned out to see her presented to the King at the Château de Saint-Cloud.

She was housed in the Jardin des Plantes (the botanical garden and zoo). Over the next few months, an incredible **600,000** visitors flocked to see her. Giraffe mania swept France. Everything was *à la girafe*: hairstyles, fabrics, porcelain, wallpaper, even biscuits were made in her image. Songs were written about her. Plays featured her. She was the ultimate fashion icon and tourist attraction.

The giraffe, later officially named Zarafa (Arabic for "charming" or "lovely"), lived in Paris for 18 years, remaining incredibly popular until her death in 1845.

Her story is a charming example of "animal chaos" in the form of mass public obsession. A single, gentle creature, sent as a political pawn, inadvertently captivated an entire nation, becoming a symbol of the exotic and sparking a cultural phenomenon unlike anything seen before.

PRESIDENT CARTER VS. THE KILLER RABBIT (USA, 1979)

It sounds like a headline from a joke newspaper: **"President Attacked by Killer Rabbit!"** But in 1979, President Jimmy Carter had a truly weird run-in with an aggressive swamp rabbit that turned into a surprisingly harmful political story.

The incident occurred in April 1979 while President Carter was taking a fishing trip in his hometown of Plains, Georgia. He was alone in a small fishing boat on a pond when, according to his account, a rabbit being chased by hounds leaped into the water and swam furiously *toward his boat.*

Carter described the rabbit as clearly distressed and behaving aggressively. He claimed it was hissing, gnashing its teeth, and paddling toward him with intent. Fearing the potentially rabid creature might try to climb into his boat, Carter did what any sensible person being charged by a swimming killer rabbit would do: He splashed water at it with his paddle.

The rabbit eventually swam away, and Carter thought nothing more of the strange encounter.

Months later, however, his press secretary, Jody Powell, mentioned the incident offhandedly to an Associated Press reporter over drinks. The reporter, Brooks Jackson, filed a story. The headline? **"President Attacked by Rabbit."**

The story exploded.

The press, and Carter's political opponents had a field day. The image of the President of the United States fending off an attack from a bunny seemed absurd, almost comical. Late-night comedians joked about it relentlessly. Cartoonists depicted Carter battling a giant, menacing rabbit. Some questioned the President's judgment or stability. Could a man spooked by a rabbit really stand up to the Soviet Union?

The White House, initially reluctant to dignify the story, eventually released an official photo taken by a staffer showing a rabbit swimming in the water near Carter's boat (though not actually attacking it). This only added fuel to the fire.

The "Killer Rabbit" incident became a symbol for critics who saw Carter as weak or hapless. It dogged him throughout the rest of his presidency and became one of those weird, sticky anecdotes that overshadowed more serious issues.

Was it really a "killer rabbit"? Probably not. Swamp rabbits *can* swim and might act erratically when fleeing predators. But the story ballooned into something far bigger—a moment of unhinged animal encounter that turned into a political liability, proving that sometimes, even a small, wet rodent can cause chaos for the most powerful person in the world.

THE HARTLEPOOL MONKEY HANGING: ESPIONAGE OR IGNORANCE? (ENGLAND, NAPOLEONIC WARS)

During wartime, fear and paranoia can run high. People see enemies everywhere. But did the residents of Hartlepool, a coastal town in northeast England, really mistake a shipwrecked monkey for a French spy and hang it? It's one of England's most enduring and bizarre local legends.

The story is set during the Napoleonic Wars (early 19th century), a time of intense conflict between Britain and France. Invasion scares were common along the coast. According to the legend, a French ship (a *chasse-marée*, or coastal trader) was wrecked during a storm off the coast of Hartlepool.

The only survivor found washed ashore was... **a monkey**.

Now, the fishermen of Hartlepool had supposedly never seen a monkey before. They had certainly never seen a Frenchman (or so the story goes). The monkey was wearing a miniature military-style uniform, likely dressed up by the French sailors for amusement—a common practice at the time.

The suspicious townsfolk interrogated the strange, hairy creature. They asked it questions in English. The monkey, naturally, couldn't understand or answer. It just chattered back in its own monkey language.

The conclusion? This small, hairy fellow in the enemy uniform, unable to speak English, must be a **French spy!**

What else could he be? Clearly, this was some kind of miniature secret agent sent by Napoleon. So, the patriotic (but maybe not smartest) people of Hartlepool held a makeshift trial right there on the beach.

The monkey was found guilty of espionage. The sentence? **Death by hanging.**

They supposedly dragged the poor creature to the town square (or used a ship's mast on the beach) and hanged it as an example to any other potential French invaders, simian or otherwise.

Is the story true? Almost certainly not in its literal details. There's no contemporary historical record of a monkey being hanged in Hartlepool. It likely originated much later, possibly as a folk song or a way for rival towns to mock the Hartlepudlians.

However, the legend stuck. People from Hartlepool are still sometimes affectionately (or insultingly) called "monkey hangers." The town's football club mascot is "H'Angus the Monkey." There's even a statue commemorating the event (depicting the monkey, not the hanging).

True or not, the legend of the Hartlepool monkey hanging is a darkly funny tale of wartime paranoia and extreme ignorance, a reminder of how fear can lead to utterly unhinged conclusions, even if it means putting a primate on trial for spying.

OPERATION ACOUSTIC KITTY:
THE CIA'S FAILED FELINE SPIES (USA, 1960S)

Espionage requires stealth, cunning, and the ability to get close to targets without raising suspicion. So, in the 1960s, during the height of the Cold War, the CIA's Directorate of Science & Technology came up with a purr-fectly logical idea: turn **cats** into sophisticated listening devices.

Thus, began **Operation Acoustic Kitty**, a top-secret project that sounds like something from a spy movie parody but was apparently quite real (though details remain classified and somewhat debated).

The concept involved surgically implanting a tiny microphone (in the cat's ear canal), a small radio transmitter (at the base of the skull), and a thin wire antenna (woven into its fur). The cat could then be let loose near Soviet officials or inside embassies, where it could wander around harmlessly while sending nearby conversations back to CIA agents. Cats are naturally stealthy, can get into places humans can't, and are generally ignored—the ideal furry bug!

The project reportedly cost millions of dollars (some estimates say up to $20 million) and took several years. Scientists and veterinarians worked on the complex surgery and miniaturized electronics. They even had to train the cats to go where they were needed, which, as any cat owner knows, is notoriously difficult. Training involved rewarding the cat for moving short distances toward specific targets.

Finally, after years of development, the first Acoustic Kitty field test was ready. The target: Two men talking on a park bench outside a Soviet compound in Washington, D.C.

CIA agents drove the specially equipped cat to the park in a van. They opened the door and released their highly trained, surgically altered, million-dollar feline spy.

The cat took a few steps out of the van, looked around, and was **immediately hit and killed by a passing taxi.**

The first mission lasted less than a minute.

According to Victor Marchetti, a former CIA officer who wrote about the project, Operation Acoustic Kitty was suddenly cancelled soon after this disastrous first try. The official conclusion was that while the science worked (they *could* turn a cat into a listening device), actually controlling the cat in a real-world environment was simply impossible. Cats, it turns out, have their own agendas.

A heavily redacted CIA memo, declassified later, confirmed the project existed, noting the technical challenges and the difficulty in training the cats to focus on their mission. It concluded, with perhaps a masterful understatement, that the program was "not practical."

Operation Acoustic Kitty remains a legendary example of Cold War espionage ambition colliding with the uncooperative reality of feline nature—an expensive, unhinged failure in the world of spycraft.

PROJECT PIGEON:
TRAINING BIRDS TO GUIDE BOMBS (USA, WWII)

If spy cats seem weird, how about **pigeon-guided missiles**? During World War II, the renowned behavioral psychologist B.F. Skinner pitched an idea to the U.S. military that was both ingenious and utterly bizarre: train pigeons to steer bombs toward enemy targets.

Skinner, famous for his work on operant conditioning (training animals using rewards), believed he could teach pigeons to recognize a target image (like an enemy ship or building) and peck at it on a screen. His proposed missile guidance system, eventually codenamed **Project Pigeon** (later Project Orcon, for "Organic Control"), worked like this:

1. A missile nose cone would be fitted with electronic screens and lenses showing an image of the ground below or ahead.

2. Three pigeons would be placed inside the nose cone, each facing a screen. (They used three pigeons just in case one messed up—the system would follow what most of them did.)

3. The pigeons would be trained with food rewards (grain) to keep pecking at the picture of the specific target on their screen.

4. If the missile started to drift off course, the target image would move off the center of the screen. The pigeons, trying to keep pecking the target, would peck off-center.

5. These off-center pecks would be detected by sensors connected to the missile's flight controls.

6. The flight controls would adjust the missile's trajectory to bring the target back to the center of the screen, where the pigeons were pecking.

Essentially, the pigeons would act as a living, pecking guidance system, keeping the missile locked onto the target until impact.

It sounds crazy, but Skinner actually demonstrated that it could work. He successfully trained pigeons to reliably track target images and keep them centered through pecking, even under simulated stressful conditions (loud noises, pressure changes). He built prototypes of the pigeon-piloted nose cone.

The military funded the project, intrigued by the possibility of creating accurate guided bombs before sophisticated electronic guidance systems were fully developed. Skinner and his team worked diligently, refining the training techniques and the hardware.

However, officials remained deeply skeptical. The idea of trusting national security to a bunch of birds seemed inherently absurd to many military leaders. Despite Skinner's successful demonstrations, the project faced constant ridicule and funding challenges.

Ultimately, the rapid development of electronic guidance systems made Project Pigeon obsolete before it could be deployed. The project was cancelled in 1944, revived briefly in 1948, and then finally scrapped for good in 1953.

While never used in combat, Project Pigeon stands as a testament to B.F. Skinner's genius in behavioral conditioning and a truly unhinged moment in military research—attempting to turn ordinary pigeons into feathered kamikaze pilots guiding bombs to their targets.

THE GREAT HORSE MANURE CRISIS OF 1894
(WORLDWIDE CITIES)

Sometimes, animal chaos isn't a single event, but a slow-motion disaster caused by the sheer number of animals involved in human life. In the late 19th century, the biggest cities in the world—London, New York, Paris—faced an environmental crisis that sounds comical today but was deadly serious then: **too much horse manure.**

Before cars, trucks, and buses took over, cities ran on horsepower. Literally. Horses pulled carriages, omnibuses (early buses), delivery wagons, streetcars, fire engines—everything. A major city like London had over 100,000 horses working its streets daily; New York had even more.

And all those horses produced... waste. A lot of it.

Estimates suggest that each horse produced somewhere between 15 to 35 pounds (7 to 16 kg) of manure per day, plus about a quart (1 liter) of urine. Multiply that by hundreds of thousands of horses, day after day, and you have a staggering problem.

- **Mountains of Manure:** Cities were literally drowning in horse dung. Streets were coated in it, often several inches deep. In dry weather, it turned into fine, foul-smelling dust that blew everywhere. In wet weather, it became a thick, slippery, disgusting sludge. Vacant lots were piled high with manure, sometimes reaching heights of 40 to 60 feet.

- **Unbearable Stench:** The smell, especially in summer, was overwhelming.

- **Disease:** Horse manure is a breeding ground for flies, which spread deadly diseases like typhoid fever. Urine soaked into the ground, contaminating water supplies.

- **Carcasses:** Horses didn't live long doing hard work in the tough city environment. Dealing with thousands of dead horse carcasses on the streets each year was another major sanitation nightmare.

- **Traffic Jams:** Just removing the manure required armies of sanitation workers (often called "street sweepers" or "mudlarks") and fleets of wagons, adding to traffic congestion.

The situation seemed unsustainable. In 1894, *The Times* of London published a grim prediction: Based on population growth and the increasing number of horses needed, by 1950, every street in London would be buried under **nine feet** of manure. Similar predictions were made for New York. Urban planners were genuinely baffled. How could cities possibly deal with the ever-growing piles of horse poop?

An international urban planning conference was held in New York in 1898 specifically to address the "Great Manure Crisis." After several days of discussion, the delegates could find no solution and abandoned the conference early, convinced the problem was insurmountable. Cities seemed doomed to suffocate under horse waste.

What saved them? Not better sanitation, but technology. The invention and mass adoption of the **automobile** in the early 20th century rapidly replaced horses for urban transport. Within a couple of decades, the horse population in cities plummeted, and the Great Horse Manure Crisis simply... vanished.

It's a strange kind of animal chaos—a crisis caused not by wild behavior, but by the sheer biological output of the animals humans relied on, a problem that seemed unsolvable until technology unexpectedly rode (or drove) to the rescue.

PART 4:

GOVERNMENT GENIUS (OR NOT!)

Governments. They make laws, build roads, collect taxes, and generally try to keep things running smoothly. Sometimes they succeed brilliantly! And other times... well, other times their plans go so spectacularly wrong, their decisions are so bafflingly weird, or their attempts at "genius" are so hilariously misguided that you just have to shake your head.

This section is dedicated to those moments of questionable government wisdom (and the occasional genuine, if strange, policy). We're talking about brilliant plans to get rid of pests that somehow result in *more* pests. We're looking at top-secret spy operations involving exploding cigars and fake radio stations inside volcanoes. We'll see governments banning fun things like football and Christmas, accidentally flooding their own parliament buildings, and causing nationwide traffic chaos just by changing which side of the road people drive on.

From financial bubbles inflated by political maneuvering to calendars that made days disappear, get ready for a tour of government actions that range from the slightly silly to the truly unhinged. Sometimes the road to chaos is paved with good intentions (and terrible planning). Let's explore some moments of "Government Genius"... or the lack thereof.

The Cobra Effect:
When Paying for Dead Snakes Gets You... More Snakes (British India)

Governments often try to solve problems with simple incentives. Want fewer pests? Offer a reward for dead pests! What could possibly go wrong?

Answer: The Cobra Effect.

The story takes place in British-ruled Delhi, India, sometime during the colonial era. The city had a problem with venomous cobras slithering around, posing a danger to residents. The British government, wanting to reduce the threat, came up with what seemed like a straightforward solution: offer a **bounty** for every dead cobra brought to them. Turn in a dead snake, get some money. Simple!

Initially, the plan worked. People eagerly hunted down cobras to claim the reward. The cobra population started to decline. Success!

But then, human ingenuity (and greed) kicked in. Some clever people realized they could make more money not just by hunting cobras, but by raising them instead.

People started setting up secret cobra farms. They'd raise cobras specifically to kill them and collect the bounty money. The government wasn't paying for *fewer* cobras in the city; they were effectively subsidizing cobra production!

Eventually, the government officials caught on to the scheme. They realized their bounty program was actually *increasing* the number of dangerous snakes, not decreasing them. So, they did the logical thing: They cancelled the bounty program.

Now, what happened to all those cobra breeders? They were stuck with farms full of venomous snakes that they could no longer sell to the government. Their inventory was worthless. So, they did the logical thing (for them): They simply **released all their now-unwanted cobras** into the city.

The final result of the government's brilliant plan to reduce the cobra population? Delhi ended up with **more** venomous cobras than before the program even started. Oops.

This situation, where trying to fix a problem accidentally makes it worse, is now known as the "Cobra Effect." It's a classic example of unintended consequences and a cautionary tale about seemingly simple government solutions backfiring spectacularly. Similar effects have been seen elsewhere, like in Hanoi, Vietnam, where a bounty on rats led to people farming rats just for their tails. It turns out, trying to outsmart nature (and human greed) isn't always as easy as it looks.

OPERATION MONGOOSE:
THE CIA'S WACKY PLOTS TO OUST CASTRO
(USA/CUBA, 1961–1962)

After the failed Bay of Pigs invasion in 1961, the U.S. government, particularly the CIA under President John F. Kennedy's administration, was obsessed with getting rid of Cuban leader Fidel Castro. This obsession led to **Operation Mongoose**, a top-secret program filled with sabotage plots, propaganda schemes, and some truly bizarre, almost cartoonish assassination ideas.

The goal was to shake up Castro's communist government and, hopefully, get rid of him for good. The CIA brainstormed endlessly, coming up with plans that ranged from the vaguely plausible to the utterly unhinged. Some of the more infamous (alleged) plots included:

- **Exploding Cigar:** Castro was known for his love of cigars. So, the CIA reportedly developed a plan to rig a cigar with enough explosives to blow his head off when he tried to light it. The cigar was supposedly prepared and even delivered to a potential contact in Cuba, but it's unclear if it ever reached Castro.

- **Poisoned Wetsuit:** Knowing Castro enjoyed scuba diving, the CIA considered contaminating a diving suit with a fungus that would cause a chronic skin disease (Maduromycosis). They also thought about rigging the breathing apparatus with tuberculosis bacteria.

- **Exploding Seashell:** Another diving-related plot involved planting an exotic seashell, large and beautiful enough to attract Castro's attention while diving, but rigged with explosives that would detonate when lifted.

- **Poison Pen:** A hypodermic needle, almost invisibly fine, would be hidden inside a ballpoint pen. An agent could supposedly bump into Castro and discreetly inject him with a potent toxin.

- **LSD Spray:** One plan involved spraying Castro's broadcasting studio with an LSD-like chemical, hoping it would cause him to have a bizarre, incoherent meltdown on air, thus discrediting him in front of the Cuban people.

- **Beard Removal Powder:** Thinking Castro's beard was key to his popular, charming image, the CIA thought about putting thallium salts (a strong hair-remover) in his shoes. The idea was that the chemical would absorb through his skin, causing his iconic beard to fall out, thus humiliating him and destroying his machismo.

Did any of these plots actually get close to working? No. Most were deemed impractical, too risky, or just plain silly, and were abandoned at the planning stage. Castro himself claimed to have survived hundreds of assassination attempts over the decades.

Operation Mongoose was eventually shut down after the Cuban Missile Crisis in 1962, as the US sought less overtly aggressive ways to deal with Cuba. But the sheer creativity and sometimes comical absurdity of the plots dreamed up during this period remain a fascinating, if slightly chilling, example of Cold War paranoia and the unhinged lengths intelligence agencies considered going to eliminate an enemy.

THE SOUTH SEA BUBBLE:
WHEN BRITAIN WENT BONKERS FOR IMAGINARY RICHES
(BRITAIN, 1720)

Governments getting involved in finance can be tricky. Sometimes it stabilizes things, other times it helps inflate massive speculative bubbles that end in disaster. The South Sea Bubble of 1720 is one of history's most spectacular examples of the latter, a nationwide frenzy of investment fueled by government deals and wild promises, ending in financial ruin for thousands.

The story starts with the **South Sea Company**, founded in 1711. The British government gave it the sole right to trade with South America (the "South Seas"). There was just one catch: South America was almost entirely controlled by Spain, and Britain was often at war with Spain. So, the actual trading potential was minimal.

But the *idea* of trading with the supposedly gold-and-silver-rich Spanish colonies captured the public imagination. The company's real purpose, however, was more complex: It was designed to help the government manage its massive national debt, incurred during various wars.

In 1720, the company proposed an audacious plan: It would take over a huge chunk of the British national debt. In exchange, holders of government debt could swap their bonds for shares in the South Sea Company, which, everyone assumed, was about to make unimaginable profits from South American trade. The government loved the idea (it made their debt look manageable), and Parliament approved the scheme.

This government backing sent South Sea Company stock prices **soaring**. Everyone wanted in on the action. Stories spread (often fueled by company insiders) about the incredible riches to be made. People from all walks of life—aristocrats, merchants, servants, farmers—poured their life savings into South Sea shares. The price went from around £128 per share at the start of 1720 to over £1,000 by August. It was pure mania.

Other ridiculous "bubble companies" sprang up, promising fortunes from equally absurd ventures (like a company "for carrying on an undertaking of great advantage, but nobody to know what it is"). People invested blindly, caught up in the frenzy.

Of course, it couldn't last. The South Sea Company had almost no real income from trade. Its value was based purely on speculation and hype. By September 1720, confidence started to crack. People realized the promised riches weren't materializing. They started selling their shares. Then more people sold. Panic set in.

The stock price **crashed**. It plummeted back down to below £200 by the end of the year. Thousands of investors, from the very rich to the very poor, were ruined. Fortunes vanished overnight. Suicides were reported. The public was furious.

A parliamentary inquiry revealed widespread fraud and corruption involving company directors and even government ministers who had accepted bribes to promote the scheme. Several politicians were disgraced.

The South Sea Bubble became a cautionary tale about the dangers of speculation, herd mentality, and the potentially disastrous consequences when government policy gets tangled up with financial market mania. It was a moment when the entire nation seemed to lose its collective mind over the promise of easy money, egged on by a government plan that prioritized financial engineering over economic reality.

FIXING THE CALENDAR:
POPE GREGORY XIII ERASES 10 DAYS (EUROPE, 1582)

Imagine waking up one morning and finding out that the date isn't what you thought it was—that the government (or in this case, the Pope) has decided to just skip the next ten days entirely. That's exactly what happened in Catholic Europe in 1582, thanks to Pope Gregory XIII and his mission to fix a drifting calendar.

The problem lay with the **Julian calendar**, introduced by Julius Caesar way back in 45 B.C. The Julian calendar calculated the year as being exactly 365.25 days long, adding a leap day every four years. This was pretty accurate, but not perfect. The actual solar year (the time it takes Earth to orbit the sun) is slightly shorter—about 365.2422 days.

This tiny difference, just about 11 minutes per year, doesn't sound like much. But over the centuries, it added up. By the 1500s, the Julian calendar had drifted by about **10 days** compared to the actual seasons. This was particularly problematic for the Catholic Church because it messed up the calculation of Easter, which was supposed to fall around the time of the spring equinox. The calendar equinox was now happening 10 days *after* the astronomical equinox.

Pope Gregory XIII decided this needed fixing, so he gathered a committee of astronomers and mathematicians, led by Christopher Clavius. They devised a new, more accurate system—the **Gregorian calendar** (the one most of the world uses today). It adjusted the rules for leap years (years divisible by 100 are *not* leap years unless they are also divisible by 400) to keep the calendar aligned with the sun over the long term.

But there was still the problem of the 10 days the Julian calendar had already drifted. The commission's solution was bold: **Just cut them out.**

Pope Gregory XIII issued a papal bull, "Inter gravissimas," decreeing that the day after Thursday, October 4, 1582, would not be Friday, October 5. Instead, it would be **Friday, October 15, 1582.**

Ten days—October 5th through October 14th—simply vanished from the calendar that year in countries that switched right away (like Italy, Spain, Portugal, and Poland).

This caused considerable confusion and chaos:

- **Rent and Wages:** Landlords worried about losing 10 days' rent. Workers worried about losing 10 days' pay.

- **Birthdays and Saints' Days:** What happened if your birthday or a favorite saint's feast day fell within the omitted period?

- **General Confusion:** Many people simply didn't understand why the dates were changing or distrusted the new system.

Protestant countries were particularly resistant. They saw the calendar change as a Catholic plot and refused to adopt it for many years, sometimes centuries. Great Britain and its American colonies didn't switch until 1752 (by which time the drift was 11 days). Russia didn't adopt it until after the Russian Revolution in 1918. This meant that for a long time, different parts of Europe were operating on completely different dates!

While the Gregorian calendar reform was scientifically necessary and ultimately successful, the abrupt removal of 10 days from existence in 1582 was a jarring, unhinged-feeling moment for ordinary people, a stark reminder that even time itself could be subject to government (or papal) decree.

BOSTON'S BIG DIG:
THE INFAMOUS MONEY PIT (USA, 1982–2007)

Sometimes, government projects aren't unhinged because they're bizarre, but because their scale, cost, and mismanagement become legendary. Boston's Central Artery/Tunnel Project, universally known as the **"Big Dig,"** is perhaps the most famous modern example of a government infrastructure project spiraling wildly out of control.

The goal was noble enough: Replace Boston's crumbling, elevated Central Artery highway (Interstate 93)—a notorious eyesore and traffic bottleneck that choked the city—with a state-of-the-art underground highway. The project also included building the Ted Williams Tunnel under Boston Harbor (connecting to Logan Airport) and the Zakim Bunker Hill Memorial Bridge over the Charles River. It was meant to transform Boston, reduce traffic, and create new parks and urban spaces where the ugly elevated highway once stood.

Planning began in the early 1980s. The initial estimated cost? Around **$2.8 billion**. The estimated completion date? **1998**.

What actually happened? It became the most expensive highway project in US history.

- **Costs Exploded:** The final official price tag ballooned to **$14.6 billion** by the time it was mostly finished in 2007. Some estimates, including debt interest, push the total cost closer to **$24 billion**. That's billions, not millions.

- **Years of Delays:** The original 1998 completion date was laughably optimistic. Major construction ran through the 1990s and early 2000s, causing constant disruption to the city. The project wasn't considered substantially complete until late 2007—nearly a decade late.

- **Design Flaws and Leaks:** The project was plagued by problems. Engineers had to navigate a maze of existing subway lines, utility pipes, and building foundations in densely packed downtown Boston. There were thousands of leaks discovered in the new tunnels, requiring extensive repairs.

- **Substandard Materials and Corruption:** Investigations revealed that some contractors had used substandard concrete and materials. There were accusations (and some convictions) related to fraud and overbilling.

- **Fatal Accident:** Tragically, in 2006, concrete ceiling panels inside one of the connector tunnels collapsed, crushing a car and killing a passenger. This led to tunnel closures, safety reviews, and further costly repairs.

The Big Dig became a national symbol of government waste, mismanagement, and infrastructure projects gone wrong. Boston residents endured years of traffic jams, noise, dust, and detours. Jokes about the never-ending project were constant.

Did it ultimately achieve its goals? Yes, mostly. The ugly elevated highway is gone, replaced by parks and development (the Rose Kennedy Greenway). Traffic flow in the city center generally improved (though some argue it just moved the bottlenecks elsewhere). The new tunnels and bridge are impressive feats of engineering.

But getting there was a crazy story of missed deadlines, unbelievable costs, and engineering nightmares, making the Big Dig a classic example of government plans crashing into the messy reality of huge building projects.

WHEN ENGLAND BANNED FOOTBALL
(VARIOUS TIMES, 14TH–17TH C)

Football (soccer) is arguably the world's most popular sport today. But back in medieval and early modern England, the government repeatedly tried to **ban** it. Why would they outlaw having a kickabout? Because the early versions of football were incredibly violent, chaotic, and interfered with more important things, like archery practice for national defense.

Medieval "folk football" wasn't like the organized game we know. It often involved entire villages or towns playing against each other. The "pitch" could be miles long, running between villages. The "goals" might be specific landmarks. There were few rules, and hundreds of people could be involved in a giant, roaming scrum.

- **It Was Violent:** Kicking, punching, wrestling, and trampling were common. Injuries happened often, and sometimes people even died. Games often turned into full-blown riots between rival villages.

- **It Damaged Property:** The massive mobs playing football would surge through fields, fences, hedges, and town streets, causing considerable damage.

- **It Distracted From Archery:** This was the biggest concern for rulers like King Edward II (who issued a ban in 1314) and King Edward III (who banned it in 1331, 1363, and 1365). England relied heavily on skilled longbowmen for its military success (especially against the French in the Hundred Years' War). The kings worried that young men were spending their Sundays playing rowdy football instead of practicing archery, weakening national security.

Kings put out orders again and again over the centuries, banning football (and other "lazy games" like tennis or dice) and telling men to practice archery instead.

Did the bans work? Not really. People loved football too much. The game continued to be played, especially in rural areas and during festivals like Shrovetide (Mardi Gras), often in defiance of the law. Enforcement was patchy.

Later bans under rulers like Henry VIII and Elizabeth I also cited the game's violence and disruption. Even King James I, who was generally more supportive of sports, disapproved of the unruly mob version of football. The Puritans under Oliver Cromwell in the 17th century also frowned upon such boisterous and "ungodly" pastimes, especially on Sundays.

It wasn't until the 19th century, when formal rules were established (often in English public schools) and the game became more organized and less violent, that football shed its reputation as a dangerous peasant pastime and started its journey toward becoming the global phenomenon it is today. But for centuries, the English government waged a losing battle against the beautiful (and formerly very brutal) game, a strange historical footnote where national security concerns led to the banning of fun.

Radio Vesuvius:
Broadcasting From Inside a Volcano (Italy, 1944)

Sometimes, government genius involves hiding in plain sight—or, in this case, hiding inside a very *unusual* sight: an active volcano. During World War II, Allied forces in Italy reportedly set up a secret radio station near the top of Mount Vesuvius to spy on German communications.

Mount Vesuvius, the famous volcano overlooking Naples and Pompeii, was technically in Allied-controlled territory after the invasion of Italy in 1943. However, German forces were still nearby, and monitoring their radio traffic was crucial.

According to stories (often told by veterans and radio fans, though official records are hard to find), a small team from the U.S. Army Signal Corps went on a daring mission. They hauled radio equipment up the slopes of Vesuvius, possibly using mules or jeeps as far as they could go, then carrying the rest. They found a suitable location—perhaps a cave, an abandoned structure, or just a well-camouflaged spot near the crater—and set up a listening post and potentially a low-power transmitter.

The location was ingenious:

- **Excellent Reception/Transmission:** High altitude generally means better radio line-of-sight.

- **Natural Camouflage:** Who would suspect a spy station operating from the slopes of an active volcano?

- **Plausible Deniability:** Any strange signals might be dismissed as atmospheric interference caused by volcanic activity.

The station, sometimes nicknamed "Radio Vesuvius," reportedly operated successfully for a period, intercepting German signals and perhaps even broadcasting misleading information or propaganda.

There was just one major occupational hazard: **the volcano itself.**

Vesuvius had been rumbling and showing signs of activity. And in March 1944, it decided to **erupt**. Not a catastrophic Pompeii-style eruption, but a significant one nonetheless, involving lava flows, ash clouds, and explosions.

The eruption forced the evacuation of nearby villages and also, presumably, the hasty dismantling and retreat of the secret radio station crew. Lava flows destroyed several villages and damaged Allied aircraft parked at a nearby airfield (coated in hot ash).

The eruption effectively ended the "Radio Vesuvius" operation. It's a small, obscure story from the vast canvas of WWII, but a wonderfully unhinged image: Allied spies huddled over radio sets, listening for German secrets, while perched precariously inside one of the world's most famous active volcanoes, only to be chased away by an inconvenient eruption. It highlights the bizarre lengths and locations involved in wartime intelligence gathering.

VOLTAIRE VS. THE LOTTERY:
HOW A PHILOSOPHER GAMED THE SYSTEM (FRANCE, 1729–1730)

Sometimes, government financial schemes have loopholes so large that clever individuals can exploit them for massive profit. In 18th-century France, the government ran a lottery designed to help pay off municipal debts. It was structured in such a way that the famous philosopher **Voltaire** and a mathematician friend figured out how to guarantee they would win almost every time.

The French government, facing significant debts, decided to issue bonds. To make these bonds more attractive, they attached a monthly lottery prize. Anyone holding a qualifying bond could buy a lottery ticket for a fraction of the bond's value (1/1000th). Each month, one lucky ticket holder would win a massive prize: 500,000 French livres—a fortune at the time.

The flaw? The government didn't consider the number of tickets sold. The prize money was fixed, regardless of how many people entered the lottery each month.

Voltaire, known for his sharp wit and philosophical writings, was also keenly interested in mathematics and finance. He discussed the lottery with a mathematician friend, Charles Marie de La Condamine. They quickly realized the loophole: If someone could buy *all* the tickets issued each month, they were guaranteed to win the 500,000-livre prize.

The cost of buying all the tickets would be significant, but *less* than the guaranteed prize money. The potential profit was huge.

Voltaire and La Condamine formed a syndicate (a group of investors). They pooled their money and recruited agents. Each month, their agents fanned out across Paris, buying up as many of the lottery tickets attached to the qualifying government bonds as they possibly could. It required careful organization and significant capital, but they managed to corner the market on tickets month after month.

And month after month, someone from their syndicate won the massive prize.

The government officials running the lottery were baffled. How could the same small group of people keep winning? They suspected cheating but couldn't figure out how. Voltaire and his partners were careful—they used different names and collected winnings discreetly. Voltaire himself once signed a winning ticket with a jokey, made-up name and address, nearly exposing the scheme when officials tried to find the "lucky winner."

The group operated successfully for almost a year, making a massive fortune (estimated at several million livres total) before the government finally caught on and stopped the lottery. Voltaire and La Condamine were brought to court, but since they hadn't technically broken any laws—they'd simply exploited a poorly designed system—they were allowed to keep their winnings.

Voltaire's lottery windfall gave him the financial independence he needed to pursue his writing and philosophical career without relying on patrons. It's a brilliant example of using mathematical logic to outsmart a flawed government scheme—a moment of "genius" exploiting a moment of government financial incompetence.

The Georgia Land Lottery: Giving Away Territory by Chance (USA, early 19th C)

Imagine the government deciding to give out huge areas of land not by selling it or through settlement rules, but by picking names from a giant wooden drum. That's essentially what the state of Georgia did in the early 19th century through a series of **Land Lotteries,** a unique and somewhat unhinged method of parceling out territory recently acquired (often forcibly) from Native American tribes like the Creek and Cherokee.

Between 1805 and 1833, Georgia held eight land lotteries. The state surveyed the newly acquired lands, divided them into standard-sized lots (varying from 40 acres to 490 acres depending on the lottery and land quality), and then distributed those lots to eligible citizens purely by chance.

Who was eligible? Generally, white men over 18 (or 21), orphans, and widows who had resided in Georgia for a certain period. Some lotteries gave extra chances to veterans or families with children. Eligible citizens would register in their home county. Their names were written on slips of paper and sent to the state capital, Milledgeville.

At the same time, slips of paper matching each available land lot (showing its district and lot number) were also made up. Blank slips were added to the mix, representing unlucky draws.

All the name slips went into one large, rotating wooden drum (called a "wheel"), and all the land lot slips (plus blanks) went into another. State officials would then simultaneously draw one name slip and one land slip. If a name was drawn with a land lot slip, that person won that specific piece of property! If a name was drawn with a blank slip, tough luck.

Why use a lottery?

- **Speed:** It was a fast way to distribute huge amounts of land quickly.

- **Perceived Fairness:** It seemed more democratic than selling land only to the wealthy or giving it to political insiders. Everyone (eligible) had a chance.

- **Encouraging Settlement:** It rapidly populated newly acquired territories with settlers, solidifying Georgia's claim to the land.

Of course, the system had its dark side. The land being given away was often taken unjustly from Native American tribes through controversial treaties or outright force, culminating in the Trail of Tears. The lottery system itself was also subject to fraud and manipulation, with insiders sometimes trying to rig the draws or gain access to desirable lots.

But the sheer concept of a state government using giant bingo drums to hand out hundreds of thousands of acres of land is a uniquely American and slightly unhinged approach to territorial expansion. It turned land ownership into a literal game of chance, shaping the settlement patterns of Georgia in a way unlike any other state.

THE PASSPORT PHOTO BAN:
TOO UGLY FOR BRITAIN? (UK, 1915)

Passports today are synonymous with those slightly awkward, often unflattering identification photos. But for a brief period during World War I, the British government actually **banned** photographs on passports, forcing people to rely solely on written descriptions. Why? Not because of security concerns, but apparently because the photos were just too variable and, frankly, often too *bad* to be useful.

The modern passport system was still developing in the early 20th century. Before WWI, passports weren't always required for international travel in Europe. The war changed everything, increasing concerns about spies, security, and border control. Britain introduced mandatory passports for all citizens traveling abroad in 1914.

Initially, these new passports included photographs of the bearer, glued onto the document. This seems logical for identification, right?

But the Foreign Office quickly ran into problems. Photography was less standardized back then. The quality, size, pose, and clarity of submitted photos varied wildly. Some people submitted glamorous studio portraits, others blurry snapshots. Lighting was inconsistent. And let's be honest, passport photos have *always* had a tendency to make people look like criminals or ghosts.

Officials apparently found these inconsistent and often terrible photos **useless for reliable identification.** They complained that the pictures rarely looked like the actual person presenting the passport. Adding to the problem, the methods for attaching photos weren't very secure, raising fears that spies could easily swap pictures.

So, in early 1915, the British government made a bizarre U-turn. They issued new regulations for passports that **eliminated the requirement for photographs.**

Instead, passports relied solely on a detailed **written description** of the bearer. This included things like height, eye color, hair color, distinguishing marks, profession, and age. The idea was that an exact written description would be more trustworthy than a photo that might be misleading or easy to fake.

Can you imagine trying to get through border control today based on a paragraph describing your "medium build" and "slightly crooked nose"? It seems absurdly inefficient and subjective.

The photo-less passport era didn't last long. Other countries continued to use photos, and the limitations of relying solely on written descriptions quickly became apparent. By the end of 1915 or early 1916 (sources vary slightly), Britain reversed course again and reinstated mandatory photographs on passports, likely with stricter guidelines for the type and quality of photo required.

But for that brief period, the British government's official position was that passport photos were so unreliable and ugly that a few descriptive sentences were a better form of identification— a strange, short-lived moment of government genius (or despair) in the history of travel documents.

CROMWELL VS. CHRISTMAS:
WHEN ENGLAND CANCELLED THE HOLIDAYS
(ENGLAND, 1640S–1650S)

Imagine a government deciding that Christmas celebrations—mince pies, carol singing, festive decorations, even taking the day off work—were illegal. That actually happened in England during the period of Puritan rule under Oliver Cromwell in the mid-17th century.

After the English Civil War (1642–1651), the victorious Parliamentarians, dominated by strict Protestants known as Puritans, effectively took control of the country. King Charles I was executed in 1649, and for a time, England was a republic (the Commonwealth), led primarily by Oliver Cromwell as Lord Protector.

Puritans had long disapproved of traditional Christmas celebrations. They believed:

- **It Was Too Catholic:** Many Christmas traditions (like carols or nativity scenes) were seen as leftovers from Roman Catholicism ("Popish superstition") that needed to be removed from the church.

- **It Was Pagan:** They argued that the date (December 25th) and many traditions (like feasting, drinking, holly, and ivy) were actually pagan in origin, co-opted by the early church, and therefore unholy.

- **It Was Wasteful and Immoral:** Puritans frowned upon the excessive eating, drinking, dancing, gambling, and general merrymaking associated with the twelve days of Christmas, seeing it as sinful, wasteful, and disorderly.

- **No Biblical Basis:** They pointed out the Bible doesn't give a date for Jesus's birth, so celebrating it on December 25th was random and not based on scripture.

Starting in the 1640s, Parliament began passing laws aimed at suppressing Christmas. An ordinance in 1644 stressed that December 25th should be kept as a day of "fasting and humiliation" for sins, not feasting. Another law in 1647 formally **abolished** the feasts of Christmas, Easter, and Whitsun (Pentecost), declaring them non-holidays.

During Cromwell's rule in the 1650s, enforcement became stricter. Shops and markets were ordered to stay open on December 25th. Soldiers were sometimes sent to patrol the streets, confiscating any festive food (especially mince pies and Christmas puddings!) they found being prepared. Churches were forbidden from holding special Christmas services. Decorations like holly and ivy were discouraged. Celebrating Christmas privately was frowned upon, and celebrating it publicly could lead to fines or punishment.

Did people obey? Not entirely. Many continued to celebrate Christmas quietly in their homes. There were even pro-Christmas riots in some cities, like Canterbury, where people protested against the forced opening of shops on Christmas Day. But officially, for over a decade, the English government tried its best to cancel Christmas.

When the monarchy was restored in 1660 with King Charles II, the anti-Christmas laws were quickly swept away, and traditional celebrations returned with gusto. But the Puritan attempt to ban Christmas remains a stark example of government overreach driven by religious ideology—a time when the state tried, and ultimately failed, to legislate merriment out of existence.

THE DEFENESTRATION OF PRAGUE:
POLITICS BY WINDOW TOSS
(BOHEMIA/CZECH REPUBLIC, 1618)

Diplomacy usually involves talking, negotiating, maybe signing treaties. In 17th-century Prague, however, unhappy Protestant nobles used a much more direct—and crazy—way to deal with the Catholic Habsburg ruler's men: **throwing them out a window.** This event, known as the Second Defenestration of Prague, wasn't just bizarre; it helped trigger one of Europe's most devastating conflicts, the Thirty Years' War.

("Defenestration" literally means the act of throwing someone or something out of a window. Prague is famous for having *three* major historical defenestrations, but the 1618 one is the most significant.)

The background was intense religious tension in Bohemia (modern-day Czech Republic). The region was largely Protestant, but it was ruled by the staunchly Catholic Habsburg Holy Roman Emperors. Emperor Matthias had promised religious tolerance, but his actions (and those of his local governors) seemed to be undermining Protestant rights, like closing down newly built Protestant chapels.

Bohemian Protestant nobles were furious. On May 23, 1618, a group of them, led by Count Thurn, stormed Prague Castle to confront two of the Emperor's representatives, the imperial governors Vilém Slavata and Jaroslav Bořita z Martinic, along with their secretary, Philip Fabricius.

The confrontation was heated. Accusations flew. The Protestants accused the governors of violating the guarantees of religious freedom. The governors defended the Emperor's actions. Arguments escalated.

Finally, the enraged Protestant nobles decided words weren't enough. They seized the two governors and their secretary. They dragged them across the room to a high window in the Chancellery building. And then, one by one, they **threw them out.**

They plummeted about 70 feet (21 meters) from the third-floor window.

Surely, such a fall onto hard ground (or pavement) would be fatal, right? That's what the Protestants probably expected. But incredibly, **all three men survived!**

How? Catholic propaganda immediately claimed it was a miracle—that angels had caught them, or the Virgin Mary had stepped in. Protestant accounts offered a more mundane explanation: They landed on a massive **pile of horse manure** and garbage that had accumulated in the dry moat below the castle wall, cushioning their fall. (The secretary, Fabricius, supposedly ran off immediately to Vienna to report the incident to the Emperor.)

Miracle or manure pile, the act itself was explosive. Throwing the Emperor's official representatives out of a castle window was a direct act of rebellion. It shattered any hope of reconciliation between the Bohemian Protestants and their Habsburg rulers.

The Defenestration of Prague is widely considered the spark that ignited the **Thirty Years' War (1618–1648)**, a brutal conflict that devastated much of Central Europe, drew in major powers like Sweden, France, and Spain, and resulted in millions of deaths.

It all started with an unhinged act of political protest—deciding that the best way to make a point to the government was not through petitions or debate, but by defenestration.

THE GREAT STINK OF LONDON:
WHEN THE THAMES BECAME A TOILET (UK, 1858)

Imagine a city smelling so bad that Parliament had to soak its curtains in disinfectant just to stand the smell, and court cases had to stop because the stink was too much. Welcome to London during the **Great Stink of the summer of 1858**, a crisis caused by centuries of government inaction and the unfortunate habit of dumping raw sewage directly into the River Thames.

For centuries, London's growing population had relied on cesspits and rudimentary drains that eventually emptied into the Thames, the city's main source of drinking water *and* its primary sewer. With the invention and popularization of the flush toilet in the mid-19th century, the problem got exponentially worse. Millions of gallons of human waste were now being flushed directly into the river every day.

The Thames became a disgusting, brown, toxic soup. It was thick with sewage, industrial effluent, and waste from slaughterhouses. The smell was appalling, especially near the riverbanks. Outbreaks of diseases like cholera, linked to contaminated water, were frequent and deadly.

For years, officials mostly ignored the problem or tinkered with ineffective solutions. But the summer of 1858 was unusually hot and dry. The water level in the Thames dropped, exposing banks of raw sewage to the baking sun. The river effectively stopped flowing, turning into a giant, fermenting cesspool.

The **stench** became unbearable. It permeated the entire city. People reportedly fainted from the fumes. It wasn't just unpleasant; it felt apocalyptic. Many believed the foul air itself (miasma) caused disease.

Crucially, the stink hit the politicians where they lived (and worked). The Houses of Parliament stand right on the banks of the Thames. MPs could barely conduct business. They tried dousing the curtains in disinfectant, considered relocating Parliament altogether, and debated endlessly about what to do. The Great Stink finally forced the government's hand.

Public outcry, combined with the politicians' own suffering, led to rapid action. Within weeks, Parliament rushed through legislation empowering engineer **Joseph Bazalgette** to build a revolutionary modern sewer system for London.

Bazalgette's plan was ambitious: construct over 80 miles of massive underground brick intercepting sewers running parallel to the Thames, collecting waste from existing drains before it reached the river. This waste would then be carried far downstream, east of the city, and discharged into the Thames estuary on the outgoing tide, safely away from London's water intakes. The project also involved building huge embankments along the Thames (like the Victoria Embankment) to house the sewers and reclaim land.

It was an enormous undertaking, taking over a decade to complete, but it worked. Bazalgette's sewers dramatically cleaned up the Thames, significantly reduced waterborne diseases like cholera, and transformed London's public health.

The Great Stink of 1858 was a moment of unhinged environmental crisis caused by government neglect, but it ultimately spurred one of the greatest public works projects of the 19th century— a stinky problem leading, eventually, to a stroke of government (and engineering) genius.

Burning the Books:
How Parliament Set Itself on Fire (UK, 1834)

Governments accumulate a lot of paperwork. Over centuries, this can become mountains of obscure, obsolete documents. In 1834, the British Parliament decided it was time for a clear-out. They needed to dispose of centuries' worth of old **tally sticks**—medieval wooden sticks used for financial record-keeping before paper became common.

Their chosen method of disposal? **Burning them** in the furnaces directly beneath the House of Lords chamber in the Palace of Westminster (the home of Parliament). What could possibly go wrong with burning huge piles of dry old wood inside the building you work in?

Tally sticks were notched pieces of wood, split lengthwise. One half was kept by the debtor, the other by the creditor (often the Exchequer, or Treasury). When a debt was paid, the two halves were matched up. By 1834, this system was long obsolete, and Parliament had amassed vast storerooms full of these old wooden records.

Officials decided the quickest way to get rid of them was incineration. On October 16, 1834, two workmen were tasked with burning cartloads of tally sticks in the furnaces of the House of Lords' heating system.

They were perhaps a little *too* enthusiastic. Instead of burning the sticks slowly over several days as advised, they reportedly overloaded the furnaces, stuffing them full of wood to get the job done quickly. The heat became intense.

The furnaces were located directly below the Lords' chamber, and the chimneys ran up through the walls of the building. The intense heat from the overloaded furnaces ignited the chimney lining. The fire then spread rapidly through the timber-framed walls, ventilation shafts, and paneled rooms of the medieval Palace of Westminster complex.

By evening, the Houses of Parliament were engulfed in a spectacular blaze. Crowds gathered along the Thames to watch the iconic buildings burn. Firefighters struggled to control the inferno.

Most of the medieval Palace of Westminster, including the chambers of both the House of Commons and the House of Lords, was destroyed. Only a few parts, like the vast Westminster Hall, survived. It was one of the biggest London fires since the Great Fire of 1666.

The cause was quickly traced back to the careless burning of the tally sticks. The government, in its attempt at bureaucratic tidiness, had accidentally burned down its own house.

The fire did have one positive outcome: It cleared the way for the construction of the magnificent neo-Gothic Palace of Westminster we know today, designed by Charles Barry and Augustus Pugin, including the famous clock tower housing Big Ben.

But the Great Fire of Parliament in 1834 remains a classic story of government incompetence—a plan to dispose of old records that went horribly wrong, leading to the destruction of centuries of history through sheer carelessness.

Dagen H:
Sweden's Chaotic Switch to Right-Hand Driving
(Sweden, 1967)

Imagine every single car in the country stopping, switching from one side of the road to the other, and then starting again, all at the same time. That's what happened in Sweden on **Dagen H** (Högertrafikomläggningen Day—"The Right-Hand Traffic Diversion Day"), September 3, 1967, when the entire country switched from driving on the left to driving on the right.

Why the switch? Most of Sweden's neighbors (like Norway and Denmark) already drove on the right. Most cars sold in Sweden were actually left-hand drive (designed for right-hand traffic), meaning drivers sat near the curb, making overtaking dangerous. With increasing cross-border traffic and car ownership, the government decided standardizing on the right side made sense for safety and convenience in the long run.

However, the Swedish public hated the idea. In a referendum in 1955, over 80% voted against switching. But the government pushed ahead anyway, believing it was necessary. They spent the next **four years** carefully planning every little detail for Dagen H.

It was a massive undertaking:

- **Infrastructure Changes:** Every single traffic sign in the country had to be reversed or replaced. Traffic lights needed reprogramming. Road markings had to be repainted. Bus stops needed moving to the other side of the road. Intersections were redesigned.

- **Vehicle Modifications:** Buses needed new doors on the right side (or were replaced). Headlights on cars needed adjusting to dip correctly for right-hand traffic.

- **Public Education Campaign:** An enormous publicity campaign was launched, using logos, songs, TV programs, radio spots, brochures, and even designs on milk cartons and underwear to constantly remind people about the upcoming switch. The "H" logo (for Högertrafik—right-hand traffic) was everywhere.

Finally, the big day arrived. Early on Sunday morning, September 3, 1967:

- **4:50 a.m.:** All non-essential traffic across Sweden was ordered to stop completely and carefully move to the right-hand side of the road.

- **5:00 a.m.:** A signal was given (often by radio), and traffic was allowed to proceed again, now driving on the right.

Chaos was widely predicted. Would drivers remember? Would there be head-on collisions everywhere?

The initial moments were tense. Traffic moved incredibly slowly and cautiously. Pictures from the time show streets jammed with cars, drivers looking confused but trying their best. There were minor fender-benders and traffic jams, especially in cities like Stockholm. Around 150 minor accidents were reported nationwide in the first few hours, though remarkably, no fatalities were directly attributed to the switch itself on Dagen H.

For weeks afterwards, driving remained slow and hesitant as people adjusted. Special low speed limits were imposed temporarily. Police were out in force directing traffic.

While Dagen H itself went relatively smoothly considering the scale of the change (thanks to the meticulous planning and the fact that it happened early on a Sunday), it was still a moment of government-mandated national chaos. Making a whole country completely change a lifelong habit overnight was a bold, maybe even crazy, achievement in managing society. It remains one of the largest logistical exercises ever undertaken by a government in peacetime.

PART 5:

CULTURAL CRAZES

Humans are social creatures. We follow trends, we copy each other, we get caught up in the moment. Usually, this is harmless stuff—fashion fads, popular songs, viral dances. But sometimes... sometimes society goes collectively off the deep end.

Welcome to the world of Cultural Crazes, where entire populations get swept up in bizarre beliefs, inexplicable behaviors, and trends so strange they defy logic. This isn't about one nutty leader or a single weird event; this is about *groups* of people, sometimes thousands or even millions, all losing their minds together in spectacular fashion.

Get ready for stories of contagious dancing plagues that couldn't be stopped, nuns meowing like cats for hours on end, financial bubbles where people traded fortunes for flower bulbs, and hoaxes that fooled entire nations. We'll meet ordinary people who declared themselves emperors (and got away with it!), explore bizarre historical jobs, witness floods of beer and molasses, and marvel at competitions that rewarded people for having the most babies.

These are the moments when common sense took a holiday, when mass hysteria gripped communities, and when the strangest ideas somehow became mainstream (at least for a little while). Let's dive into the weird world of cultural crazes and see just how strange things can get when people follow the crowd.

EMPEROR NORTON I:
THE MAN WHO DECLARED HIMSELF RULER OF AMERICA
(USA, 1859–1880)

Imagine declaring yourself Emperor of the United States after losing your fortune. Now imagine the city you live in just... playing along. Meet Joshua Norton, a San Francisco businessman who did just that in 1859. After a disastrous attempt to corner the rice market left him broke and possibly mentally shaken, he walked into the offices of the *San Francisco Bulletin* newspaper on September 17, 1859, and handed them a proclamation: "At the peremptory request and desire of a large majority of the citizens of these United States, I, Joshua Norton... declare and proclaim myself Emperor of these United States..." He later added "Protector of Mexico" for good measure.

Instead of being ignored or locked up, Norton became a beloved city character. Dressed in a donated blue military uniform with gold epaulets and often sporting a beaver hat adorned with feathers or flowers, he spent his days inspecting the city's streets, cable cars, and the condition of public buildings. He issued further decrees in the newspapers—grandly "abolishing" the U.S. Congress (for corruption), dissolving the Democratic and Republican parties, ordering the construction of a suspension bridge connecting Oakland and San Francisco (remarkably predicting the Bay Bridge's eventual location), and levying fines against anyone caught using the disrespectful nickname "Frisco."

The truly unhinged part wasn't just Norton's delusion, but how San Francisco embraced him:

- **His Own Money:** He printed "Imperial Treasury Bond Notes," typically in denominations of 50 cents to $10, promising 7% interest upon redemption (which never happened). Astonishingly, many San Francisco restaurants, bars, theaters, and shops accepted these notes as payment, often displaying them proudly afterwards.

- **Free Perks:** Norton often dined for free in establishments that displayed brass plaques reading "By Appointment to his Imperial Majesty Emperor Norton I." Theaters reserved balcony seats for him and his two stray dogs, Lazarus and Bummer (who were themselves minor city celebrities). He rode public transport without charge, and the Presidio army post regularly supplied him with replacement uniforms when needed.

- **Public Respect:** People generally treated him with respect, bowing or tipping their hats. Police officers would salute him. When a rookie cop made the mistake of arresting Norton in 1867 (for vagrancy or his mental state), public outrage was swift and fierce. Newspapers strongly criticized the arrest. The police chief, Patrick Crowley, quickly ordered Norton's release, issued a formal apology from the police force, and ensured Norton had a carriage ride home. From then on, police officers saluted Norton whenever they encountered him. The city directories even began listing his occupation as "Emperor."

When Emperor Norton collapsed on the street and died in January 1880, the city genuinely mourned. Initial reports painted him as a pauper, but searches revealed he had a small amount of cash, his valuable collection of walking sticks, letters from foreign monarchs (real or imagined), and his imperial hats. His funeral was arranged by the Pacific Club, a prestigious businessmen's association. An estimated **30,000 people**—nearly 10% of the city's population, from millionaires to paupers—lined the streets for his funeral procession. The *San Francisco Chronicle*'s headline read *"Le Roi est Mort"* ("The King is Dead"). Emperor Norton's story is a bizarre, heartwarming tale of a city choosing kindness over ridicule, turning one man's harmless delusion into a beloved local legend.

THE TORONTO STORK DERBY:
BABY-MAKING FOR BIG BUCKS (CANADA, 1926–1936)

What if having the most babies could make you rich? That was the premise of the Great Stork Derby in Toronto, sparked by the mischievous will of a wealthy lawyer. Charles Vance Millar, an eccentric, childless bachelor known for his practical jokes, died in 1926. His will contained several pranks, but the most sensational was Clause 9: The bulk of his fortune (worth millions in today's money) was to be held in trust for ten years, then given "to the mother who has since my death given birth in Toronto to the greatest number of children."

This triggered a decade-long **baby-making race** (October 31, 1926–October 31, 1936). During the worst of the Great Depression, the chance for a life-changing fortune pushed families into a desperate race. The media dubbed it the "Stork Derby" and breathlessly tracked the leading contenders. Public health officials fretted about the toll on mothers' health and the welfare of children potentially born just to win the prize. The rules seemed simple—live births in Toronto within the timeframe—but complications arose. Stillbirths didn't count. What about babies who died shortly after birth? And crucially, did the children have to be legitimate? The will didn't specify, leading to intense moral debates and legal wrangling.

When the ten years were up in 1936, chaos ensued. Several mothers stepped forward. Two families, those of Annie Katherine Smith and Kathleen Ellen Nagle, were tied with ten births each, but some of their children were tragically stillborn, potentially disqualifying them. Other mothers, like Lillian Kenny and Lucy Timleck, had nine children who clearly met all criteria. The case landed in court amidst intense public interest. Lawyers argued over the definition of "child," the validity of the will itself, and the thorny issue of legitimacy.

Finally, in 1938, a judge delivered the verdict. The prize money, which had grown significantly with interest, was divided primarily among **four mothers**—Lillian Kenny, Lucy Timleck, Kathleen Nagle, and Isabel MacLean—each of whom had produced **nine eligible live children**. They each received over $100,000, a staggering sum at the time. Two other mothers with strong claims were awarded smaller consolation prizes due to technicalities. The Stork Derby remains one of history's strangest contests, a bizarre social experiment fueled by a prank will and the desperation born of poverty.

THE DANCING PLAGUE OF 1518:
WHEN PEOPLE DANCED THEMSELVES TO DEATH
(STRASBOURG)

Imagine dancing uncontrollably for days, even weeks, joined by hundreds of others, until some collapse and die from exhaustion. This nightmare scenario wasn't fiction; it gripped the city of Strasbourg (then part of the Holy Roman Empire) in the summer of 1518. It reportedly began in July with one woman, known as Frau Troffea. She stepped into the street and began to dance fervently, silently, and intensely. She didn't stop for nearly a week.

Within days, others began to join her compulsive movements. By the end of the first week, over 30 people were dancing. Within a month, the number had swelled to an astonishing **400 people**. The city was in the grip of an inexplicable dance marathon.

Baffled authorities, desperate for an explanation, consulted local physicians. Ruling out supernatural causes, they landed on a diagnosis of "hot blood"—essentially, overheated brains. Their prescribed cure seems utterly insane today: **more dancing!** Believing the dancers needed to dance the fever out, officials cleared open spaces, put up a wooden stage, and even hired musicians and professional dancers to keep the sufferers moving.

This strategy backfired disastrously. The public spectacle and rhythmic music seemed only to draw *more* people into the involuntary frenzy. The scene became a grotesque street party, hundreds flailing, jumping, and twirling day and night, unable to control their own bodies. The physical toll was horrific. People danced until their feet were bloody stumps. They suffered dehydration, exhaustion, heart attacks, and strokes. Contemporary accounts claim that at the plague's peak, up to 15 people per day were literally dying from dancing.

Realizing their catastrophic error, the authorities reversed course. They banned public dancing, dismantled the stages, and transported the afflicted to shrines to pray for divine intervention, particularly the shrine of Saint Vitus, patron saint against neurological disorders (hence the phenomenon sometimes being called "St. Vitus's Dance"). The plague eventually subsided sometime in late August or early September.

What caused this madness? Theories abound: **mass psychogenic illness** triggered by the extreme stress of recent famine and disease; **ergotism**, poisoning from a hallucinogenic fungus on rye bread (though this usually restricts blood flow, making dancing difficult); or perhaps an extreme, uncontrolled **religious cult ritual**. Whatever the trigger, the Dancing Plague remains a terrifying and deeply unhinged example of collective hysteria.

THE PLAGUE DOCTOR'S OUTFIT: TERRIFYING BEAKS AND SWEET SMELLS (EUROPE, 17TH C ONWARD)

That iconic, creepy image of a historical plague doctor—the long dark coat, wide-brimmed hat, gloves, and the terrifying bird-like beak mask—wasn't just a flight of fancy. It was a real uniform worn by some physicians treating bubonic plague victims, particularly from the 17th century onward. Developed by Charles de Lorme, physician to French royalty, the outfit was based entirely on the flawed **miasma theory**—the belief that diseases like the plague were spread by "bad air" or poisonous vapors.

Every part of the costume aimed to block this invisible enemy:

- **Beak Mask:** The most crucial element. The long beak (often 6 inches or more) wasn't just for intimidation; it was a primitive respirator stuffed with aromatic herbs, spices, dried flowers, camphor, or vinegar-soaked sponges (common ingredients included mint, cloves, myrrh, rose petals, ambergris, and laudanum). The idea was that these strong, nice smells would filter out or cancel the deadly "bad air" before the doctor breathed it in. Glass eyepieces allowed sight through the fragrant barrier.

- **Waxed Coat:** They thought a heavy, ankle-length coat made of waxed leather or canvas couldn't be penetrated by the bad air. The slick surface might also have discouraged fleas (which we now know actually carried the plague bacteria, Yersinia pestis) from latching on.

- **Gloves, Boots, Hat:** Leather gloves protected the hands, boots covered the feet, and a wide-brimmed leather hat offered slight additional protection and perhaps denoted the wearer's profession.

- **Wooden Cane:** This served multiple purposes: examining patients from a distance without touching them (to avoid miasma contamination), directing family members or assistants, pushing away desperate crowds who might try to grab the doctor, and sometimes even for taking a pulse or lifting clothing.

Did the suit actually protect the doctors? Not from miasma, which didn't exist. It might have offered some minimal protection against flea bites simply due to the amount of coverage, but the aromatic beak was useless against bacteria. However, the psychological impact was immense. Imagine being desperately ill, and the person arriving to "cure" you looks like a terrifying omen of death emerging from a nightmare. The plague doctor's outfit became a potent symbol of fear, death, and the bizarre, unhinged medical theories of the past.

GROOM OF THE STOOL:
THE KING'S ROYAL WIPER
(ENGLAND, TUDOR AND STUART ERAS)

Think your job involves getting close to the boss? Try being the **Groom of the King's Close Stool** in Tudor and Stuart England (roughly 15th to 18th centuries). This wasn't a joke; it was one of the most prestigious, intimate, and surprisingly powerful positions at the royal court. The job description? Assisting the King with his toilet duties—essentially, being the official royal bottom-wiper and chamber pot attendant. The "Close Stool" itself was a portable toilet, often an ornate chair or box containing a pot.

Why was such a seemingly menial task so highly sought-after? **Access.** Unparalleled, intimate access. The Groom saw the King at his most vulnerable and unguarded moments, often being the first person the King spoke to in the morning and the last at night. This proximity allowed for informal conversation, the sharing of state secrets, and the unique opportunity to influence the monarch's opinions and decisions away from the formal pressures of the council chamber.

The job was therefore saved for high-ranking noblemen who were close personal friends and trusted advisors of the King. It came with a generous salary, luxurious apartments within the palace, powerful perks, and significant political influence. The Groom often managed the King's private finances (the Privy Purse) and acted as a de facto personal secretary, controlling access to the King's private chambers (the Privy Chamber). Courtiers seeking favors, appointments, or simply the King's ear often had to curry favor with the Groom of the Stool first.

Famous Grooms included Sir William Compton under Henry VIII (who became wealthy and powerful) and Sir Anthony Denny (who was present at Henry VIII's deathbed and may have influenced the signing of his final will). The role gradually became less hands-on and more ceremonial over time, eventually evolving into the "Groom of the Stole" (referring to a ceremonial robe). But for centuries, one of the most influential figures in the English court was the man responsible for the King's bowel movements—a bizarre cultural quirk highlighting vastly different historical notions of privacy, status, and the corridors of power.

THE GREAT LONDON BEER FLOOD: A TSUNAMI OF STOUT (UK, 1814)

Floods usually involve water. But on October 17, 1814, the impoverished London neighborhood of St. Giles was devastated by a sudden, deadly flood of **beer**. The source was the Meux and Company Brewery on Tottenham Court Road, which housed enormous wooden vats for fermenting porter, a popular dark beer. One gigantic vat, over 22 feet high and holding about 135,000 gallons, suddenly burst its iron hoops.

The explosion triggered a catastrophic domino effect, smashing other vats and demolishing the brewery's thick brick wall. A **15-foot wave of dark, frothing beer** surged into the densely packed slum streets of the St. Giles Rookery. The force was immense, instantly destroying two houses and flooding the cellars of many others where poor families lived. People were trapped by the rapidly rising alcoholic tide, crushed by debris, or drowned in the dark liquid.

Chaos ensued. While some rushed to rescue victims, others reportedly saw the river of free beer as an unexpected bounty, scooping it up in any available container or even drinking straight from the flood. The aftermath was tragic: eight people died, mostly women and children trapped in basements. The brewery lost a ton of money but didn't have to pay taxes on the lost beer after an official investigation called the disaster an "Act of God." The Great London Beer Flood remains one of history's strangest and deadliest industrial accidents.

ANNE BONNY AND MARY READ:
FEMALE PIRATE POWER COUPLE (CARIBBEAN, ~1720)

The "Golden Age" of Caribbean piracy (early 18th C) was a brutal, male-dominated world. Yet two women, **Anne Bonny** and **Mary Read**, defied all expectations to become infamous pirates, fighting fiercely alongside the crew of Captain "Calico Jack" Rackham.

Anne Bonny, fiery and Irish-born, ditched her sailor husband for Rackham and joined his crew, initially disguised as a man but later fighting openly. Mary Read, English-born, spent much of her life disguised as a boy, even serving as a soldier, before being captured by Rackham's pirates and joining them as "Mark Read."

The unhinged twist, according to Captain Charles Johnson's (not always reliable) pirate history: Anne, unaware Mary was female, developed a crush on "Mark." When Anne revealed her own gender, Mary was forced to reveal hers too! Instead of rivalry, they became close friends and fighting partners. When Rackham grew jealous, Mary revealed her secret to him as well. Both women became known for being incredibly fierce in battle, often leading the attack while the men held back.

Their careers ended with Rackham's capture in 1720. The men were swiftly hanged. Anne and Mary, however, avoided immediate execution by "pleading their bellies"—revealing they were pregnant. Mary died in prison soon after, possibly from fever. Anne's fate is a mystery; some say she was ransomed and lived a long life, others that she vanished. Their story is still a thrilling tale of women rebelling against the strict rules about how men and women should act back then.

PRESIDENT TAFT GETS STUCK: THE BATHTUB INCIDENT (USA, ~1909–1913)

William Howard Taft, the 27th US President (1909–1913), was a notably large man, with his weight reportedly exceeding 300 pounds during his presidency. Because of his size, one of the longest-lasting and funniest presidential stories started: **He got stuck in a White House bathtub.**

The popular story claims that Taft, shortly after moving in, became wedged in the standard-sized bathtub and required assistance from several staff members to be extricated. While there's no solid proof this actually happened—it might be a made-up story spread through political gossip because of Taft's size—what *is* undeniably true is that Taft subsequently ordered a **massive, custom-built bathtub** for the White House.

This replacement tub was enormous: over seven feet long and 41 inches wide, crafted by the J. L. Mott Iron Works. Photos exist showing four workmen comfortably sitting inside it before installation. Whether prompted by an embarrassing incident or simply a desire for a comfortable bath, the existence of this gigantic presidential tub cemented Taft's association with bathroom fixtures in popular culture, making it a uniquely unhinged historical detail.

THE GREAT PYRAMID WATER SLIDE SCANDAL
(EGYPT/MEXICO, 1977)

Turning the 4,500-year-old Great Pyramid of Giza into a game show prop seems unthinkable, but Mexican TV producer Roberto Arnavit tried it in 1977. For his popular show *"El gran premio de los 64,000 pesos"*, he planned a spectacular stunt: attaching a **giant water slide** to the side of the ancient monument for contestants.

Incredibly, Arnavit secured some form of initial permission from Egyptian authorities (perhaps due to miscommunication) and began assembling scaffolding and slide sections near the pyramid's base. Once the full, audacious plan became public—running water down the priceless monument—**fury erupted** across Egypt. The potential damage and sheer disrespect were appalling.

The Egyptian government swiftly intervened, halting the project immediately and reportedly ejecting Arnavit and his crew from the country. The incident became a cautionary tale about protecting world heritage sites from commercial exploitation and truly harebrained ideas, a thankfully aborted plan to turn an ancient wonder into a temporary water park.

THE GREAT CANADIAN MAPLE SYRUP HEIST
(CANADA, 2011–2012)

Canada's **Strategic Maple Syrup Reserve** in Quebec, managed by the Federation of Quebec Maple Syrup Producers, holds millions of pounds of syrup to stabilize prices. It's like Fort Knox, but for breakfast topping. Between 2011 and 2012, this reserve was hit by a bold robbery: Thieves stole almost **3,000 tons** of syrup worth **$18.7 million CAD.**

This sophisticated, inside job unfolded over months. Thieves gained access to a reserve warehouse, secretly transported barrels of valuable syrup to a remote sugar shack, siphoned it off, refilled the original barrels with **water**, and returned them to avoid detection. The stolen syrup was gradually trucked out and sold on the black market across Canada and the US.

The massive theft was only discovered during a routine inventory in fall 2012 when an inspector found suspiciously light barrels. The scale was stunning—about 10% of the entire reserve. A major police investigation led to over 25 arrests, exposing a complex network. The "Great Canadian Maple Syrup Heist" remains a uniquely Canadian and absurdly unhinged crime story.

THE MEOWING NUNS OF FRANCE
(FRANCE, MIDDLE AGES)

Mass hysteria can manifest in truly bizarre ways. One strange case, reported by later chroniclers (so details may be exaggerated), occurred in a medieval French convent where nuns inexplicably began **meowing like cats**. According to the story, it started with one nun, but the behavior spread contagiously until the entire convent gathered daily at a set time to meow in unison for several hours.

The constant, disturbing caterwauling baffled the surrounding community. Eventually, soldiers were reportedly called to intervene. Faced with threats (perhaps of whipping or other punishment), the nuns abruptly ceased their collective meowing. Explanations range from **mass psychogenic illness** brought on by the stresses of confined religious life, to religious extremism, or even a strange form of communal boredom or rebellion. Though historical proof is thin, the tale of the meowing nuns endures as a striking example of unhinged collective behavior.

THE GREAT MOLASSES FLOOD:
BOSTON DROWNS IN SWEETNESS (USA, 1919)

On an unseasonably warm January 15, 1919, Boston's North End experienced a disaster stranger than fiction: a deadly flood of **molasses**. A huge storage tank owned by the Purity Distilling Company, 50 feet tall and holding over 2.3 million gallons of raw molasses, suddenly burst open. Rivets popped like machine guns, and the steel walls gave way.

A **25-foot wave of thick, heavy molasses** burst outwards at an estimated 35 mph. It flattened buildings, buckled the elevated railway, and engulfed streets, horses, and people in a sticky tide 1.5 times denser than water. 21 people were killed (crushed or suffocated), and 150 were injured. Rescue efforts were nightmarish, as the goo acted like quicksand. The harbor turned brown, and the neighborhood reportedly smelled sweet for decades after. Shoddy construction and thermal expansion were blamed. It remains one of America's most bizarre and tragic industrial disasters.

THE GREAT DIAMOND HOAX OF 1872: FOOLING THE EXPERTS (USA)

In 1872, cousins Philip Arnold and John Slack pulled off a bold scam, convincing some of America's richest guys they'd found a huge diamond field out West. They arrived in San Francisco, deposited rough gems at a bank, and hinted at a secret discovery, luring investors like Bank of California founders and associates of Tiffany & Co.

After being paid around $600,000 (millions today), they agreed to take the investors' chosen expert, renowned geologist **Clarence King**, to the site—blindfolded for part of the journey. In remote northwestern Colorado, King found a landscape seemingly littered with diamonds and other gems. Despite some doubts, the sheer abundance and geological setting largely convinced him, sparking diamond fever back east.

However, King's lingering suspicions led him to return alone. He noticed gems that don't occur together naturally, and a diamond showing signs of being cut. He realized the cousins had **"salted"** the site with thousands of cheap, imported, uncut gems. King exposed the fraud in November 1872, crashing the investors' company. Arnold and Slack vanished with the money. The hoax proved even top experts could be fooled by greed and a well-crafted craze.

THE GREAT MOON HOAX OF 1835:
LIFE FOUND ON THE LUNAR SURFACE! (USA)

Could newspapers announce life on the Moon and get away with it? In 1835, the New York *Sun* did just that. Seeking to boost circulation, it published six sensational articles supposedly reprinted from a Scottish science journal, detailing discoveries by famed astronomer Sir John Herschel using a new super-telescope in South Africa.

The articles vividly described lunar forests, oceans, bison-like creatures, blue unicorns, and, most stunningly, winged, furry, human-like **bat-men** ("Vespertilio-homo") who built temples and conversed! The public went wild. *The Sun*'s circulation became the world's highest. Other papers reprinted the stories. Debates raged.

Of course, it was **completely fake**. Herschel saw no bat-men; the Scottish journal was defunct. Reporter Richard Adams Locke likely wrote it as satire or a stunt. The hoax unraveled within a week, but surprisingly, the public was mostly amused rather than angry. *The Sun* kept its readers. The Great Moon Hoax is still a classic example of the media tricking people and how easily a wild story could start a craze before anyone could check the facts.

Tulip Mania: When Flower Bulbs Cost More Than Houses (Netherlands, 1634–1637)

One of history's earliest and most bizarre speculative bubbles centered on... **tulip bulbs**. In the 1630s Dutch Republic, tulips imported from Turkey became the ultimate status symbol. Rare varieties, especially those with striking "broken" patterns (caused by a virus), were highly prized.

From 1634 to early 1637, prices exploded. It wasn't just the rich; people from all classes began speculating, trading bulbs and futures contracts (promises to buy bulbs later) for insane profits. Prices became utterly detached from the bulbs' real value. At the peak (winter 1636–1637), a single rare bulb like *Semper Augustus* could fetch the price of an Amsterdam canal house or vast estates. People invested life savings and traded property for flowers.

In February 1637, the bubble burst. Confidence vanished overnight. Buyers disappeared, panic selling ensued, and prices crashed, sometimes to less than 1% of their peak value. Fortunes were wiped out, bankruptcies followed, and the Dutch economy shuddered. Tulip Mania became the classic warning story about crazy investing, a time when a whole country lost its mind gambling on flower bulbs.

PART 6:

OTHER WILD STORIES

We've journeyed through ridiculous wars, met leaders who lost their minds, witnessed animal chaos, questioned government genius, and explored bizarre cultural crazes. But history's weirdness doesn't fit neatly into boxes. Some stories are just too strange, too unique, or too mysterious to categorize.

This final section is a collection of those tales—the historical odds and ends, the truly unhinged moments that defy easy labels. We're talking about disasters involving collapsing floors and cesspits, incredible tales of survival against impossible odds, medical mysteries that lasted decades, unsolved disappearances, coded messages we still can't crack, and hints of contact from beyond our world.

These are the stories that make you go "Wait, what?!" one last time. From deadly snowballs to laughing epidemics, from marathon runners who took half a century to finish to pirates who became national heroes, get ready for one final dive into the weirdest corners of the past. Let's explore the best of the rest in unhinged history!

THE ERFURT LATRINE DISASTER:
A ROYAL FLUSH OF NOBLES (GERMANY, 1184)

Royal meetings are usually formal, maybe tense. They don't typically end with dozens of nobles drowning in a giant toilet. But that's the Erfurt Latrine Disaster of 1184. King Henry VI of Germany called a meeting in Erfurt's Petersberg Citadel to settle a feud between two powerful nobles. The second-floor hall was packed with counts, dukes, and bishops.

Suddenly, the aging wooden floor **collapsed**. Everyone in the meeting plunged into the giant cesspit below—a deep pit full of years' worth of sewage. Imagine the horror: Europe's elite submerged in liquid filth. Many drowned instantly or were killed by falling debris. Chroniclers report around **60 deaths**, a catastrophic loss.

Ironically, the two feuding nobles survived by clinging to window ledges. King Henry VI also survived, possibly saved by sitting in a stone alcove. Shaken and disgusted, the King quickly left Erfurt, the feud overshadowed by the sheer, stinking horror of nobles drowning in a medieval latrine.

Tsutomu Yamaguchi:
The Man Who Survived Two Atomic Bombs
(Japan, 1945)

Being hit by an atomic bomb is unimaginably horrific. Surviving one is miraculous. Surviving *two* seems utterly impossible. Yet, that's exactly what Japanese engineer Tsutomu Yamaguchi did during the final days of World War II.

Yamaguchi, a young naval engineer working for Mitsubishi Heavy Industries, was in **Hiroshima** on a business trip on August 6, 1945. He was preparing to leave the city when, around 8:15 a.m., he saw a B-29 bomber drop a small object attached to a parachute. Then came a blinding flash of light—the "Little Boy" atomic bomb detonating.

Yamaguchi was less than two miles from ground zero. The blast threw him into the air, burst his eardrums, temporarily blinded him, and badly burned the left side of his upper body. Despite his injuries, he managed to find his way to an air-raid shelter, spent the night there amidst the devastation, and found two colleagues who had also survived.

Wanting desperately to get home to his wife and infant son, the injured Yamaguchi and his colleagues made their way through the ruined city to the train station the next day. They managed to board one of the few trains still running, heading toward his hometown: **Nagasaki**.

He arrived in Nagasaki on August 8th, wounded, bandaged, and deeply shaken. He went to a hospital, then reported back to his Mitsubishi office on August 9th to tell his disbelieving boss about the single bomb that had destroyed Hiroshima.

He was in the middle of describing the blinding flash and deafening boom he'd witnessed just three days earlier when, around 11:02 a.m., an even brighter white light filled the Nagasaki office. The "Fat Man" plutonium bomb had detonated over the city.

Yamaguchi was again about two miles from ground zero. Miraculously, despite being exposed to the second atomic blast within 72 hours, his injuries this time were less severe (though his existing bandages were ruined, and he suffered a high fever for weeks from the double dose of radiation). His office building was heavily damaged, but he survived.

Even more incredibly, he rushed home through the newly devastated city to find that his wife and son, who had been out shopping for burn ointment for him, had also miraculously survived the Nagasaki bombing with relatively minor injuries.

For decades, he rarely spoke publicly about his experience. However, later in life, he spoke out strongly for getting rid of nuclear weapons, sharing his unique story to show how horrible they are. The Japanese government officially recognized him as a *nijū hibakusha* (double-bomb survivor) in 2009, shortly before his death from stomach cancer in 2010 at the age of 93.

While there were other known survivors of both bombings, Tsutomu Yamaguchi is the only person officially recognized by Japan as having endured the full horror of both atomic attacks and lived to tell the tale—an almost unbelievable story of survival against impossible odds.

CHARLES OSBORNE:
THE 68-YEAR HICCUP ATTACK
(USA, 1922–1990)

Most people get the hiccups for a few minutes, maybe an hour at most. It's annoying, sometimes embarrassing, but it passes. Now imagine hiccuping continuously for **68 years**. That was the unbelievable reality for Charles Osborne of Anthon, Iowa.

Osborne's epic hiccup ordeal began in 1922. He was working on a farm, attempting to weigh a 350-pound hog for butchering. As he lifted the heavy animal, he fell. He felt fine afterwards, but shortly after the fall, he started hiccuping. And he didn't stop.

Doctors were baffled. Osborne saw many different doctors and specialists over the years. They tried various cures, from breathing into paper bags to hypnosis to pressure point techniques. Nothing worked. One doctor attempted a surgery involving severing a small nerve related to breathing, which silenced the hiccups temporarily but posed life-threatening risks, so it wasn't pursued further. Another doctor managed to stop the hiccups by treating Osborne with carbon monoxide, but Osborne couldn't tolerate the treatment long-term.

So, he learned to live with it. For the next **68 years**, Charles Osborne hiccuped relentlessly. Initially, the hiccups came at a rate of about 40 times per minute, later slowing to around 20 times per minute. Doctors estimated he hiccuped roughly **430 million times** over his lifetime.

How did he cope? Remarkably well, all things considered. He learned to minimize the "hic" sound by breathing techniques between spasms. He continued to work as a farmer and later as a farm machinery salesman. He got married twice and had eight children. People said he kept a positive attitude even though he was dealing with this constant problem. Eating was challenging; he often had to blend his food in later years to avoid choking during a hiccup spasm.

His condition earned him a place in the *Guinness Book of World Records* for the longest continuous hiccup attack. He appeared on radio shows and television programs like *Ripley's Believe It or Not!* and *That's Incredible!*

Then, one morning in February 1990, Osborne woke up, and the hiccups were simply... gone. For no apparent reason, after 68 years, they stopped. He was finally able to live hiccup-free.

Sadly, he only enjoyed about a year of silence. Charles Osborne died in May 1991 from complications related to ulcers, just shy of his 97th birthday. His 68-year bout of hiccups remains the longest ever recorded, a bizarre medical mystery and a testament to one man's incredible endurance in the face of a relentless, unhinged bodily function.

SHIZO KANAKURI:
THE MARATHON RUNNER WHO TOOK 54 YEARS
(SWEDEN/JAPAN, 1912–1967)

Running a marathon is tough. Finishing one takes endurance and determination. But what about taking **54 years, 8 months, 6 days, 5 hours, 32 minutes, and 20.3 seconds** to complete the race? That's the incredible (and slightly misleading) story of Shizo Kanakuri, a Japanese marathon runner at the 1912 Stockholm Olympics.

Kanakuri was one of Japan's first Olympic athletes, a promising long-distance runner. He traveled to Stockholm for the Games, a long trip by ship and train that reportedly took him 18 days and left him tired out. Race day itself, July 14, 1912, was unexpectedly hot, reaching temperatures that were challenging for marathon runners at the time.

The race was grueling. Many runners dropped out due to the heat. One Portuguese runner, Francisco Lázaro, tragically collapsed and died the next day—the first death during a modern Olympic event. Kanakuri also struggled immensely. Somewhere around the halfway mark, suffering from hyperthermia (overheating) and exhaustion, he stopped at a house along the course where spectators were offering refreshments. He accepted some juice, sat down for a moment... and fell asleep.

He reportedly slept for several hours (some accounts say a whole day!). When he woke up, he was deeply ashamed. He felt he had disgraced himself and his country by failing to finish the race. Instead of telling race officials he was quitting, Kanakuri quietly left the house and, with friends' help, went back to Japan without letting the Olympic officials know.

Back in Sweden, Kanakuri was simply listed as "missing." His disappearance became a minor Olympic mystery. Had he gotten lost? Had something happened to him? Nobody knew.

Life went on. Kanakuri became known as the "father of marathon running" in Japan, helping to establish popular long-distance races like the Hakone Ekiden relay. He competed in two more Olympics (1920 and 1924) but never achieved his earlier promise. He lived a long life as a geography teacher.

Fast forward to **1967**. Swedish television decided to track down the "missing" runner from the 1912 Games as part of the 55th anniversary celebrations of the Stockholm Olympics. They found Kanakuri, now 75 years old and retired, living in Japan.

They invited him back to Stockholm. In a charming and symbolic gesture, they gave him the opportunity to finally **finish the race** he had started 54 years earlier. Kanakuri jogged the final stretch into the historic Stockholm Olympic Stadium, crossing the finish line.

When his time was announced—54 years, 8 months, etc.—Kanakuri reportedly joked, "It was a long trip. Along the way, I got married, had six children, and 10 grandchildren."

Shizo Kanakuri's story is a quirky and heartwarming tale of Olympic history, a testament to perseverance (even if interrupted by a half-century nap), and a reminder that sometimes, finishing the race takes a little longer than expected.

Hunt Brothers:
Trying to Corner the World's Silver (USA, 1979–1980)

In 1979, wealthy Texas oil heirs Nelson Bunker Hunt and William Herbert Hunt tried to corner the **global silver market**. Believing silver was safer than paper money due to inflation, they, along with Saudi partners, bought up massive amounts of physical silver and futures contracts, estimated at **half the world's deliverable supply**.

Their buying frenzy drove silver prices from $6/ounce to nearly **$50/ounce** by January 1980, causing chaos. People sold silverware, industrial costs soared, and financial markets shuddered. Regulators intervened, changing rules on the commodity exchanges (like COMEX) by sharply increasing margin requirements and allowing "liquidation only" trading.

The Hunts couldn't meet the massive margin calls. On **"Silver Thursday"** (March 27, 1980), their brokers started dumping their silver. The price collapsed by over 50% in a day. The crash threatened banks and brokerages. The Hunts lost billions, faced lawsuits and fines, and eventually filed for bankruptcy. Their unhinged gamble remains a legendary tale of financial hubris.

Oxford vs. Cambridge Snowball Riot (England, 1381)

Student rivalries can sometimes get out of hand. But a snowball fight blowing up into a full-blown armed riot involving townspeople and university officials? That happened during the tumultuous **Peasants' Revolt** in England in 1381, involving students from Oxford and Cambridge.

The Peasants' Revolt was a major uprising across large parts of England, fueled by economic hardship, high taxes (following the Black Death and wars with France), and social unrest. While centered on peasants and artisans, the chaos provided opportunities for other groups to settle scores or vent frustrations.

In Cambridge, tensions were already high between the university scholars ("town vs. gown" rivalry was common). During the broader revolt sweeping the nation in June 1381, a group of Cambridge townspeople, perhaps emboldened by the general lawlessness, attacked university property and personnel. They reportedly burned university records and charters, trying to erase the privileges and debts owed to the university.

Meanwhile, some Cambridge scholars decided to flee the troubled town. A group of them headed toward Oxford, perhaps seeking refuge or simply trying to get away. Along the way, near the town of High Wycombe, they encountered a group of **Oxford scholars.**

What started next is unclear—perhaps old rivalries flared, perhaps there was a misunderstanding. But according to some stories, the meeting broke down into **a massive snowball fight**. (Yes, in June! Weather patterns were different, or perhaps "snowball" was a euphemism, or maybe the timing detail is slightly off in the chronicles.)

Whatever the projectiles, the fight quickly escalated beyond snowballs. Both groups of scholars were likely armed (traveling was dangerous). Swords were drawn; arrows may have been fired. The student brawl turned bloody.

Local townspeople from High Wycombe, possibly resentful of scholars in general, joined in, siding against the students. The situation devolved into a chaotic riot. Several scholars were reportedly killed or seriously injured.

The incident, though small compared to the main Peasants' Revolt events happening elsewhere, highlights the intense rivalries and simmering violence that could exist between student bodies and between universities and local communities in medieval England. A snowball fight turning into an armed riot with fatalities? Definitely an unhinged moment in academic history.

MOUNT TAMBORA AND THE YEAR WITHOUT A SUMMER (INDONESIA/GLOBAL, 1815–1816)

Natural disasters can be crazy because of how huge they are and the surprising things they cause. The eruption of **Mount Tambora** in Indonesia in April 1815 was the largest volcanic eruption in recorded human history, and its effects were felt across the globe, leading to the bizarre and miserable **"Year Without a Summer"** in 1816.

Tambora, located on the island of Sumbawa, exploded with unimaginable force. The eruption column reached over 25 miles high, spewing out vast quantities of ash, rock, and sulfur dioxide gas into the atmosphere. The explosions were heard hundreds of miles away. Pyroclastic flows (fast-moving currents of hot gas and volcanic debris) devastated the surrounding island, killing tens of thousands of people instantly or through subsequent starvation and disease as crops were destroyed. It remains the deadliest volcanic eruption in recorded history.

But the impact didn't stop there. The huge amount of volcanic ash and sulfur spray shot into the stratosphere spread around the world, causing a kind of **volcanic winter**. These particles formed a veil that partially blocked sunlight, causing global temperatures to drop significantly.

The result was the **Year Without a Summer** in 1816. Weather patterns went completely haywire, particularly in the Northern Hemisphere:

- **Europe:** Experienced cold, rainy, and gloomy conditions throughout the summer. Crops failed across Britain, Ireland, France, and Germany, leading to food shortages, riots, and famine. It was the worst famine in 19th-century mainland Europe. Rivers froze in summer. Brown and reddish snow was reported in Italy.

- **North America:** Saw bizarre cold snaps and snow during June, July, and August in New England and Eastern Canada. Frosts killed off crops repeatedly. Farmers faced ruin. People called it "Eighteen Hundred and Froze to Death." Migration westward accelerated as people fled the harsh conditions.

- **Asia:** The eruption disrupted the Asian monsoon season, leading to flooding in some areas (like India, possibly triggering a new strain of cholera) and crop failures elsewhere (like China).

The strange, gloomy weather even had cultural impacts. Stuck indoors during a cold, wet summer vacation by Lake Geneva in Switzerland, a group of writers, including Lord Byron, Percy Bysshe Shelley, and Mary Shelley, held a ghost story competition. Mary Shelley was inspired by the bleak atmosphere (and scientific discussions about galvanism) to begin writing her masterpiece, **Frankenstein**. Lord Byron wrote his poem "Darkness," reflecting the apocalyptic mood. The gloomy conditions are also thought to have influenced the landscape paintings of J.M.W. Turner.

The eruption of Mount Tambora was a natural event of unhinged power, triggering a global climate anomaly that caused widespread suffering, famine, and bizarre weather, leaving a lasting mark on human history and culture.

THE GREAT PANTS REBELLION
(FRANCE, 16TH CENTURY)

Fashion disputes rarely lead to armed conflict, but in 16th-century France, attempts by the nobility to regulate what peasants could wear—specifically, fancy pants—reportedly sparked actual resistance, sometimes dubbed the **"Great Pants Rebellion."**

Laws limiting spending on fancy clothes, food, or furniture based on social class (called sumptuary laws) were common in medieval and Renaissance Europe. They aimed to maintain the social hierarchy, prevent lower classes from imitating nobles, and curb excessive spending.

In France, these laws often targeted specific garments. One particularly contentious item was **breeches** or **hose** (what we might think of as tights or fitted trousers). As fashion evolved, breeches became more elaborate, colorful, and sometimes "puffed" or "slashed" with expensive fabrics showing through—styles favored by the aristocracy.

When peasants or lower-class townspeople started adopting these fancier styles, the nobility got upset. It blurred the lines of social distinction. So, authorities periodically issued or reinforced laws forbidding commoners from wearing certain types or colors of luxurious breeches, silks, or other high-status clothing items.

According to some historical accounts and local legends (details can be hard to pin down precisely), these "pants laws" didn't always go over well. In certain regions or towns, attempts to enforce these restrictions met with **violent resistance**.

Imagine tax collectors or local officials trying to fine or punish a peasant for wearing overly colorful or "poofy" pants, only to be met by an angry mob of fellow pants-wearers armed with farm tools! While perhaps not a single, unified "Great Pants Rebellion," there were likely numerous localized incidents where commoners literally fought for their right to wear the clothing they chose, seeing the sumptuary laws as unjust and oppressive.

These weren't just fashion statements; they were assertions of personal freedom and dignity against an aristocratic elite trying to dictate every aspect of life, right down to the style of one's trousers. It's a bizarre but telling example of how even clothing could become a battleground for social conflict in the past.

Jean Lafitte:
Pirate Hero of New Orleans
(USA/Gulf Coast, ~1810–1815)

Can a notorious pirate, smuggler, and slave trader become a national hero? In the case of **Jean Lafitte** during the War of 1812, the answer is a surprising yes. Lafitte and his band of buccaneers, operating out of the swamps and bayous of Louisiana, played a crucial, if unlikely, role in helping the United States defeat the British at the Battle of New Orleans.

Lafitte was a shadowy figure, likely born in France or its Caribbean colonies. By the early 1800s, he and his brother Pierre were leaders of a large group of privateers-turned-pirates known as the "Baratarians," based in Barataria Bay, south of New Orleans. They preyed on Spanish ships in the Gulf of Mexico (often selling captured goods and slaves illegally in New Orleans), dodging both Spanish and American authorities. Lafitte created an image for himself as a charming, classy gentleman, even while running a huge smuggling operation.

When the War of 1812 broke out between the US and Britain, Lafitte was in a tricky position. The U.S. governor, William Claiborne, distrusted him and wanted to shut down his operation. The British, however, saw Lafitte's strategic location and experienced fighters as a potential asset.

In 1814, British naval commanders approached Lafitte with a tempting offer: Join them in their upcoming attack on New Orleans, and they would reward him with land, money, and a captaincy in the Royal Navy. They also threatened to destroy his base if he refused.

Lafitte appeared to consider the offer but was secretly playing for time. He despised the Spanish (Britain's allies) and felt some loyalty (or perhaps saw more opportunity) with the Americans. He sent word of the British offer and their attack plans to the American authorities in New Orleans.

Governor Claiborne initially dismissed Lafitte's warning. But General **Andrew Jackson**, arriving to take command of the city's defenses, was more pragmatic. Jackson desperately needed trained artillerymen and ammunition to defend New Orleans against the impending British invasion. Lafitte had both.

Despite his official condemnation of the pirates, Jackson met with Lafitte. A deal was struck: Lafitte and his Baratarians would fight for the Americans. In return, Jackson promised to seek official pardons for their past crimes.

During the decisive Battle of New Orleans in January 1815, Lafitte's men proved invaluable. Their expert cannoneers manned several key artillery batteries, pouring devastating fire into the advancing British ranks. They also provided crucial supplies of gunpowder and flint. The American victory was overwhelming, securing the Mississippi River and boosting national morale.

True to his word, Andrew Jackson praised the Baratarians' courage and secured presidential pardons for Jean Lafitte and his men. For a short, amazing time, the pirate was praised as a hero who played a key part in saving New Orleans.

Lafitte's heroic status didn't last forever. He eventually returned to his shadowy dealings in the Gulf, possibly engaging in piracy again, and disappeared from historical record around 1823. But his unlikely alliance with Andrew Jackson remains a uniquely unhinged episode where a wanted criminal became a celebrated patriot overnight.

TANGANYIKA LAUGHING EPIDEMIC (TANZANIA, 1962)

Mass hysteria isn't just a medieval phenomenon. In 1962, in the newly independent nation of Tanganyika (now part of Tanzania), a bizarre epidemic broke out, not of dancing or meowing, but of uncontrollable **laughter and crying**.

The outbreak began on January 30, 1962, at a mission-run boarding school for girls in the village of Kashasha. It reportedly started with three girls, who began laughing uncontrollably. The laughter quickly spread to other students. It wasn't joyful laughter; it was often accompanied by crying, restlessness, and sometimes pain or fainting. Attacks could last from a few minutes to several hours.

The laughter became so widespread and disruptive—affecting 95 out of the 159 students aged 12–18—that the school was forced to close down in mid-March. But closing the school only spread the problem.

Students went home to their villages, and the "laughing sickness" spread to other communities. It affected primarily adolescents but also some adults. Another school had to be closed. In total, the epidemic lasted for months, spreading sporadically through several villages and affecting perhaps over **1,000 people**. Some reports suggest it took nearly 18 months for the phenomenon to completely die out.

What caused this strange outbreak? Medical investigations at the time found no evidence of physical illness, infection, or environmental toxin. The prevailing theory today is that it was a case of **mass psychogenic illness (MPI)**, or mass hysteria, likely triggered by stress.

The students at the mission school were reportedly under considerable pressure from demanding teachers and high expectations. The transition to independence in Tanganyika may also have created underlying social stress. The initial laughter incident, perhaps triggered by a joke or minor event, could have acted as a release valve, and the behavior then spread contagiously through shared stress and social mimicry within close-knit communities.

The Tanganyika Laughing Epidemic is still one of the best-recorded modern examples of mass hysteria, a weird and crazy reminder that mental stress can sometimes show up in strange, hard-to-explain group behaviors that spread like a virus.

CLAUDETTE COLVIN:
THE TEENAGER BEFORE ROSA PARKS (USA, 1955)

Nine months *before* Rosa Parks's famous act, 15-year-old **Claudette Colvin** refused to give up her bus seat to a white passenger in Montgomery, Alabama, on March 2, 1955. She argued her constitutional rights, was forcibly dragged off the bus by police, and arrested.

Civil rights leaders considered using Colvin's case to challenge segregation but ultimately chose Parks. Why? Colvin was young and seen as emotional. Crucially, she became pregnant shortly after her arrest, and leaders feared this would be used to discredit the movement. Rosa Parks, older and with an impeccable reputation, became the symbol.

Though largely forgotten by mainstream history, Colvin was one of four plaintiffs in **Browder v. Gayle,** the federal case that ruled bus segregation unconstitutional, ending the Montgomery Bus Boycott. Her story is a vital piece of unfiltered history about youth activism and difficult strategic choices.

THE LOST COLONY OF ROANOKE:
AMERICA'S OLDEST UNSOLVED MYSTERY (USA, 1590S)

In the late 16th century, England made its first serious attempts to establish a permanent colony in North America. Sir Walter Raleigh sponsored several expeditions to Roanoke Island, off the coast of present-day North Carolina. The final attempt, established in 1587 and led by Governor John White, ended in one of America's most enduring and unhinged mysteries: The entire colony vanished without a clear trace.

The 1587 colony consisted of over 115 men, women, and children, including Governor White's own daughter, Eleanor Dare, who gave birth to Virginia Dare—the first English child born in the New World. Running low on supplies, Governor White sailed back to England later that year to get more help, planning to come back quickly.

However, his return was delayed for **three years** due to England's war with Spain (specifically, the Spanish Armada crisis of 1588, which required all available ships for defense).

When White finally managed to return to Roanoke Island in August 1590, he found the settlement completely **deserted**. There were no signs of a struggle, no bodies, no definitive clues about what had happened to the colonists. The houses had been dismantled, indicating an orderly departure, not a panicked flight or attack.

The only physical clue left behind was the word **"CROATOAN"** carved into a post of the fort's palisade, and the letters **"CRO"** carved into a nearby tree.

Croatoan was the name of a nearby island (modern-day Hatteras Island) and also the name of a local Native American tribe friendly to the English. Before leaving in 1587, White had instructed the colonists that if they had to move, they should carve their destination onto a tree or post. He also told them to carve a Maltese cross above the name if they were leaving under duress or danger. There was no cross.

White assumed the colonists had simply relocated to Croatoan Island to live with the friendly tribe. Bad weather prevented him from sailing south to investigate immediately, and he was forced to return to England. Later trips to find the colonists either failed or never actually happened.

With no definitive answers, the Roanoke colonists simply vanished from history, leaving behind only the cryptic carving "CROATOAN" and centuries of speculation—America's oldest unsolved mystery.

THE VOYNICH MANUSCRIPT: HISTORY'S MOST MYSTERIOUS BOOK (15TH C?)

Imagine a medieval book filled with elegant handwriting and intricate illustrations, but written in a language or code that **no one**—not top cryptographers, linguists, or historians—has ever been able to decipher. That's the **Voynich Manuscript**, a centuries-old enigma that has baffled experts and fueled endless speculation.

Named after Wilfrid Voynich, the Polish book dealer who acquired it in 1912, the manuscript is a codex (an early type of book) handwritten on vellum (animal skin). Carbon dating suggests the vellum dates to the early 15th century (1404–1438). Its history before Voynich acquired it is murky, though it may have passed through the hands of Holy Roman Emperor Rudolf II, alchemists, and Jesuit scholars.

What is it? Theories range wildly:

- An unknown natural language or a constructed artificial language.

- An elaborate cipher or code hiding a known language.

- A hoax created to fool a wealthy collector (like Emperor Rudolf II).

- The ravings of a madman or the work of an outsider artist.

- An alchemical text, a medical treatise, an herbal guide, or a religious text from an unknown sect.

Despite countless attempts, the Voynich Manuscript guards its secrets. It sits in Yale University's Beinecke Rare Book & Manuscript Library, a beautiful, confusing, and totally bizarre object that still won't give up its secrets.

THE DYATLOV PASS INCIDENT:
UNEXPLAINED MOUNTAIN DEATHS (RUSSIA, 1959)

In the winter of 1959, nine experienced hikers set out on a challenging expedition in the remote Ural Mountains of the Soviet Union. They never returned alive. When search parties found their campsite and bodies weeks later, the scene was so bizarre and terrifying that it sparked decades of speculation and conspiracy theories, known as the **Dyatlov Pass Incident**.

The group, mostly students from the Ural Polytechnical Institute, led by Igor Dyatlov, aimed to reach Otorten Mountain. They were all skilled skiers and hikers, well-equipped for the harsh conditions. They set up camp on the slopes of Kholat Syakhl (meaning "Dead Mountain" in the local Mansi language) on the night of February 1st or 2nd.

Then, something catastrophic happened.

Investigators found the hikers' tent **slashed open from the inside**. Their belongings—boots, warm clothing, equipment—were left neatly inside. Footprints in the snow showed the hikers had fled the tent in a state of panic, heading downhill toward a nearby forest, despite temperatures well below freezing (-25 to -30 °C or -13 to -22 °F). Shockingly, many of them were barefoot or wearing only socks or a single boot.

The first two bodies were found near the tree line, about a mile from the tent, next to the remains of a small fire. They were dressed only in their underwear. Three more bodies (including Dyatlov's) were found between the tree line and the tent, seemingly having tried to return uphill.

Further bizarre details emerged:

- Some of the hikers' clothing contained **significant levels of radiation**.

- Witnesses (including other hikers and meteorologists) reported strange **orange spheres or lights** in the sky in that area around the time of the incident.

- The official Soviet investigation vaguely decided the hikers died from some **powerful natural force** they couldn't handle.

What happened? Theories range from the plausible to the wildly unhinged:

- **Avalanche:** Did a small avalanche hit the tent, causing panic and internal injuries? (But why cut the tent from inside? Why no external trauma? Why flee so far downhill, partially clothed?)

- **Infrasound:** Could wind passing over the mountain create low-frequency infrasound, inducing panic and irrational behavior?

- **Military Weapons Test:** Were they accidentally killed by a secret Soviet weapon test? (Explaining radiation and lights?)

- **Paradoxical Undressing:** Did severe hypothermia cause them to feel hot and irrationally remove clothing? (Possible, but doesn't explain the injuries or fleeing the tent.)

- **Animal Attack:** Unlikely, as no animal tracks were found, and the injuries weren't typical.

- **Attack by Mansi tribesmen:** Also, unlikely; the Mansi were peaceful, and the injuries weren't consistent with a human attack.

- **UFO/Alien Encounter or Yeti Attack:** The most outlandish theories, fueled by the strange lights and injuries.

The Dyatlov Pass Incident remains officially unsolved, a chilling mystery filled with bizarre clues and unhinged possibilities, haunting the remote slopes of Dead Mountain.

THE WOW! SIGNAL:
A MESSAGE FROM OUTER SPACE? (USA, 1977)

Are we alone in the universe? The Search for Extraterrestrial Intelligence (SETI) uses radio telescopes to listen for signals from potential alien civilizations. On August 15, 1977, astronomer Jerry Ehman, working with Ohio State University's "Big Ear" radio telescope, detected something amazing: A strong, focused radio signal that seemed excitingly like it could be the message from the stars people had been looking for.

The Big Ear telescope scanned the sky, and its output was recorded on continuous computer printouts. While reviewing the data days later, Ehman spotted an incredibly strong signal sequence in the printout from August 15th. Radio signals from space usually have specific characteristics if they are artificial rather than natural. This signal ticked several boxes:

- **Narrowband:** It occupied a very narrow range of frequencies, typical of artificial transmissions, unlike natural sources, which tend to broadcast over wider bands.

- **Frequency:** It was very close to the **hydrogen line** (1420 MHz), a frequency astronomers theorized aliens might use for interstellar communication because hydrogen is the most common element in the universe.

- **Strength:** It was incredibly strong—over 30 standard deviations above the background noise, far louder than typical cosmic static.

- **Pattern:** It lasted for 72 seconds, the exact duration expected for a fixed signal source being scanned by the Big Ear telescope as the Earth rotated. It rose and fell in intensity exactly as predicted for an extraterrestrial signal passing through the telescope's beam.

Ehman was so stunned by the signal's characteristics, which perfectly matched expectations for an intelligent alien broadcast, that he circled the corresponding alphanumeric code on the printout ("6EQUJ5") and wrote **"Wow!"** in the margin. The name stuck.

What happened next? Intense excitement, followed by frustrating silence. Astronomers, including Ehman, repeatedly scanned the same patch of sky where the signal originated (in the constellation Sagittarius). They used the Big Ear and other, more powerful radio telescopes.

They found **nothing**. The Wow! signal was never detected again.

What was it?

- **An Alien Broadcast:** The signal's characteristics remain the best fit for an intentional, non-natural transmission from an extraterrestrial source. But why was it never repeated? Was it a one-off beacon? Did we just happen to be listening at the exact right moment?

- **Earth-Based Interference:** Could it have been a stray signal from a satellite, aircraft, or ground-based transmitter reflecting off space debris? Possible, but the signal's frequency was in a protected band reserved for radio astronomy, where terrestrial transmissions are forbidden. Extensive checks failed to find any known Earthly source.

● **Undiscovered Natural Phenomenon:** Could some rare, unknown natural astrophysical event mimic an artificial signal so perfectly? Highly unlikely, according to most experts, but not entirely impossible.

● **Instrument Glitch:** Also considered unlikely given the signal's duration and pattern matching the telescope's scan.

The Wow! signal is still the best possible candidate ever found for a message from aliens, but where it came from is a complete mystery. It's a 72-second cosmic mystery, a tantalizing, unhinged blip in the data that makes us wonder: Did someone, or something, out there say "Wow!" back?

CONCLUSION

And... scene! You've officially survived a whirlwind tour through the most bizarre, baffling, and downright bonkers corners of history. Give yourself a round of applause (or maybe just check if any pigeons nearby are trying to guide missiles).

We've seen armies fight birds (and lose), leaders try to appoint horses to high office (and maybe succeed?), bears join the army, governments accidentally cause snake plagues while trying to *prevent* snake plagues, entire towns dance themselves to death, and people pay more for flower bulbs than for houses. We've encountered exploding whales, killer bunnies, pickled ears that started wars, corpses put on trial, and strategic reserves of... maple syrup?

If your brain feels slightly scrambled, congratulations! That means you were paying attention.

Hopefully, you've realized that history isn't just a boring list of dates, names, and treaties droned on about in stuffy classrooms. It's a chaotic, hilarious, often deeply weird story made by people who were, let's be honest, frequently making things up as they went along, often with disastrous or just plain strange results.

The stories you learned in school? That was just the highlight reel—the polished, sensible version. But the *real* history, the unhinged history, is often way more interesting (and way funnier). It's full of moments that make you slap your forehead, question reality, and wonder how humanity managed to stumble its way to the present day.

So, what now? Don't let the weirdness stop here! History is *full* of these kinds of stories, hiding just beneath the surface. Keep asking questions. Dig deeper than the textbook. Look for the footnotes, the weird local legends, the plans that went spectacularly wrong. Find the stories that make you think, "Wait, did that *really* happen?!"

Because chances are, it probably did.

Now go out there knowing that the past was way more unhinged than you ever imagined. Impress your friends. Annoy your teachers. And never, ever trust a calm-looking rabbit near a fishing boat. Stay curious!

REFERENCES

A brief moment of history: When Napoleon took on rabbits. (2023, January 27). Just History Posts. https://justhistoryposts.com/2023/01/27/a-brief-moment-of-history-when-napoleon-took-on-rabbits/

Anastasi, L. (2023, December 23). *Pope Formosus' trial in the Cadaver Synod.* Medieval History. https://historymedieval.com/pope-formosus-trial-in-the-cadaver-synod/

Andrews, E. (2025, January 30). *What was the dancing plague of 1518?* History. https://www.history.com/news/what-was-the-dancing-plague-of-1518

Borrell, B. (2013, January 4). The great Canadian maple syrup heist. *Bloomberg Businessweek.* https://www.bloomberg.com/news/features/2013-01-02/the-great-canadian-maple-syrup-heist

The Cadaver Synod: When the Catholic Church dug up a dead pope to put his corpse on trial. (n.d.) History Skills. https://www.historyskills.com/classroom/ancient-history/cadaver-synod/

Dorman, P. F. (2025, April 15). Akhenaten. *Encyclopedia Britannica.* https://www.britannica.com/biography/Akhenaten

Emu War. (n.d.). In *Wikipedia.* Retrieved May 5, 2025. https://en.wikipedia.org/wiki/Emu_War

Evans, K. (n.d.). *Canute and the waves: A misunderstood story.* Kelly Evans – Author. https://kellyaevans.com/nqhistory/waves-2/

Fetterley, J. (2021, July 6). *King Canute.* Perennial Wisdom with Judith Fetterley. https://www.perennialwisdom.net/king-canute/

Galeano, E. (n.d.). *July 14, 1969: Soccer war.* Zinn Education Project. https://www.zinnedproject.org/news/tdih/soccer-war/

Goldstein, R. (2010, January 9). Hiroo Onoda, soldier who hid in jungle for decades, dies at 91. *The New York Times.* https://www.nytimes.com/2014/01/18/world/asia/hiroo-onoda-imperial-japanese-army-officer-dies-at-91.html

Gore, J. G. (2016, October 18). Looking back: Australia's Emu Wars. *Australian Geographic.* https://www.australiangeographic.com.au/topics/wildlife/2016/10/australias-emu-wars/

Graboyes, E. M., & Hullar, T. E. (2013, July). The War of Jenkins' Ear. *Otology & neurotology: official publication of the American Otological Society, American Neurotology Society [and] European Academy of Otology and Neurotology, 34(2),* 368–372. https://pmc.ncbi.nlm.nih.gov/articles/PMC3711623/

Jeremiah, O. (n.d.) *The war that lasted 335 years - without a single shot fired. Vocal Media.* https://vocal.media/history/the-war-that-lasted-335-years-without-a-single-shot-fired

Johnson, A. (2022, November 20). *Caligula the mad emperor: The horse that almost became a senator and other strange tales.* Museum Hack. https://museumhack.com/caligula-mad-emperor/

Johnson, M. (2006). 'Feathered foes': Soldier settlers and Western Australia's 'Emu War' of 1932. *Journal of Australian Studies, 30*(88), 147–157. https://doi.org/10.1080/14443050609388083

Kulik, R. M. (2025, January 14). Emu War. *Encyclopedia Britannica.* https://www.britannica.com/topic/Emu-War

The life & legend of Emperor Norton. (2025). The Emperor Norton Trust. https://emperornortontrust.org/emperor/life

Martin, D. (2009). *Emperor Norton I: The rise of a San Francisco cultural icon 1859-1880.* Western CEDAR. https://cedar.wwu.edu/cgi/viewcontent.cgi?referer=&httpsredir=1&article=1020&context=wwuet

Matthews, C. (2021, May 8). World's longest and weirdest war between the Isles of Scilly and the Netherlands. *Cornwall Live.* https://www.cornwalllive.com/news/cornwall-news/story-behind-worlds-longest-weirdest-4092887

Meddings, A. (n.d.). *Caligula – the mad emperor who declared war on the sea.* Walks Inside Rome. https://www.walksinsiderome.com/blog/caligula-war-on-the-sea/

Murtoff, J. (n.d.). *Wojtek the bear.* https://www.britannica.com/animal/Wojtek-the-Bear

The 1969 'Soccer War' between Honduras and El Salvador. (n.d.). Association for Diplomatic Studies and Training. https://adst.org/2014/06/the-1969-soccer-war/

O'Connor, T. (2022, October 14). *Our Legal Heritage: Gregory IX, the cat-killing pope who laid down the law.* https://www.irishlegal.com/articles/our-legal-heritage-gregory-ix-the-cat-killing-pope-who-laid-down-the-law

Perro, P. (n.d.). *King Canute.* https://www.history-for-kids.com/king-canute.html

Reilly, L. (n.d.). The time Napoleon was attacked by rabbits. *Mental Floss.* https://www.mentalfloss.com/article/51364/time-napoleon-was-attacked-rabbits

Ryan, C. (2024, June 11). *The Roman Emperor Caligula declared war on the sea.* NavalHistoria. https://navalhistoria.com/the-roman-emperor-caligula-declared-war-on-the-sea/

Soth, A. (2019, February 7). The Cadaver Synod: Putting a dead pope on trial. *JSTOR Daily.* https://daily.jstor.org/the-cadaver-synod-putting-a-dead-pope-on-trial/

Suetonius. (2007). *The twelve Caesars* (R. Graves, Trans.; M. Grant, Rev.). Penguin Classics. (Original work c. 121 CE)

Tampashrew. (ca. 2013). *Did Caligula really declare war on Neptune?* [Online forum post]. Reddit. https://www.reddit.com/r/AskHistorians/comments/1rsslc/did_caligula_really_declare_war_on _neptune/

Taronas, L. (n.d.). *Akhenaten: The mysteries of religious revolution.* ARCE. https://arce.org/resource/akhenaten-mysteries-religious-revolution/

That one time Napoleon was attacked by rabbits. (2023, May 17). Ripley's Believe It or Not!. https://www.ripleys.com/stories/attacked-by-rabbits

U.S. Senate Select Committee to Study Governmental Operations With Respect to Intelligence Activities. (1975). *Alleged assassination plots involving foreign leaders: An interim report (Report No. 94-465).* U.S. Government Printing Office. https://www.intelligence.senate.gov/sites/default/files/94465.pdf

Voynich Manuscript. (n.d.). Beinecke Rare Book & Manuscript Library, Yale University. https://beinecke.library.yale.edu/collections/highlights/voynich-manuscript

When the famous Carthaginian general Hannibal catapulted poisonous snakes at enemy ships. (n.d.). History Skills. https://www.historyskills.com/classroom/ancient-history/hannibal-snake-bombs/

Who is Joshua Norton, a South African immigrant who once declared himself emperor of the United States? (2025, April 20). The Economic Times. https://economictimes.indiatimes.com/news/international/global-trends/who-is-joshua-norton-a-south-african-immigrant-who-once-declared-himself-emperor-of-the-united-states/articleshow/120459824.cms?from=mdr

Wikipedia. (n.d.). Cadaver Synod. In *Wikipedia.* Retrieved April 26, 2025. https://en.wikipedia.org/wiki/Cadaver_Synod

Wikipedia. (n.d.). Exploding whale. In *Wikipedia.* Retrieved April 6, 2025. https://en.wikipedia.org/wiki/Exploding_whale

www.ingramcontent.com/pod-product-compliance
Lightning Source LLC
Chambersburg PA
CBHW070118030426
42335CB00016B/2194